D1001268

"I have never read such a penetrating exploration of China's e-commerce scene. Not only does it cover the unique characteristics of China's e-commerce landscape but it also delves into the cultural motivators of the Chinese people who are uniquely passionate about online shopping."

Tom Doctoroff, CEO,
J Walter Thomson Asia,
author of *Billions* and *What Chinese Want*

"Inquisitive and well-articulated, East-Commerce *describes in a unique way how China is leapfrogging the West in many key online sectors – a must read."*

John Lindfors,
Managing Partner and Director,
DST Investment Management,
former Partner Goldman Sachs

"East Commerce *provides incredible insight into the technological and cultural changes going on in China. It is especially valuable for multinational companies doing business in China to re-frame their thinking and marketing approach and to build loyalty in this massive market."*

Chandos Quill,
VP Global Data Solutions, Merkle Inc

"East-Commerce *gives an insider's perspective on what it's like to operate in the biggest e-commerce market in the world – each one of my team members has this book on their desk."*

Bruno Feltracco,
VP and Managing Director,
The North Face Asia Pacific

"Marco Gervasi delivers crucial insight into the global implications associated with the increasing relevance and reach of the 'East- Commerce' model."

Michael Injaychock,
Sr. Director, Touchpoint Optimization,
Eli Lilly and Company

"East-Commerce *reads more like a novel than a text book as it details the evolution of the Chinese ecommerce marketplace and offers great insight into how to successfully navigate the complicated landscape."*

Richard Russell,
Director Media Strategy,
Deckers Outdoor Corporation

East-Commerce

A JOURNEY THROUGH CHINA E-COMMERCE AND THE INTERNET OF THINGS

Marco Gervasi

WILEY

This edition first published 2016
© 2016 Marco Gervasi

This is a revised edition of East-Commerce: A Journey Through China E-Commerce and the
Internet of Things, published 2015

Registered office
John Wiley & Sons Ltd, The Atrium, Southern Gate, Chichester, West Sussex, PO19 8SQ,
United Kingdom

For details of our global editorial offices, for customer services and for information about how
to apply for permission to reuse the copyright material in this book please see our website at
www.wiley.com.

All rights reserved. No part of this publication may be reproduced, stored in a retrieval system,
or transmitted, in any form or by any means, electronic, mechanical, photocopying, recording
or otherwise, except as permitted by the UK Copyright, Designs and Patents Act 1988, without
the prior permission of the publisher.

Wiley publishes in a variety of print and electronic formats and by print-on-demand. Some
material included with standard print versions of this book may not be included in e-books or
in print-on-demand. If this book refers to media such as a CD or DVD that is not included in
the version you purchased, you may download this material at http://booksupport.wiley.com.
For more information about Wiley products, visit www.wiley.com.

Designations used by companies to distinguish their products are often claimed as trademarks.
All brand names and product names used in this book are trade names, service marks,
trademarks or registered trademarks of their respective owners. The publisher is not associated
with any product or vendor mentioned in this book.

Limit of Liability/Disclaimer of Warranty: While the publisher and author have used their best
efforts in preparing this book, they make no representations or warranties with respect to the
accuracy or completeness of the contents of this book and specifically disclaim any implied
warranties of merchantability or fitness for a particular purpose. It is sold on the understanding
that the publisher is not engaged in rendering professional services and neither the publisher
nor the author shall be liable for damages arising herefrom. If professional advice or other
expert assistance is required, the services of a competent professional should be sought.

A catalogue record for this book is available from the Library of Congress.

A catalogue record for this book is available from the British Library.

ISBN 978-1-119-23088-5 (hardback)

Cover design: Wiley
Background image: barbaliss/Shutterstock
Horse image: © Shelby Chen

Set in 11/13pt NewBaskervilleStd-Roman by Thomson Digital, Noida, India
Printed in Great Britain by TJ International Ltd, Padstow, Cornwall, UK

Contents

Foreword

It often takes an outside eye to help us more clearly see where we are, and where we could be going. But Marco Gervasi is no outsider. He is one of those rare individuals able to thrive within the borders of both East and West, linking together the realms of business and technology to extract a broader view of what is happening in global technology.

In December of 2014, I co-hosted the first *IDEAS Summit on the Internet of Things and Humans*, in Shenzhen, China. Marco and I were lucky enough to share a dinner table, and it was there that he described to me the book he was writing on China's e-commerce industry and the Internet of Things (IoT).

Marco had already interviewed an impressive array of thought and industry leaders across China and Asia. And so our conversation naturally led to many others, wherein I rapidly realized that what Marco was writing was a seminal analysis on China's technological development to date. By writing this foreword, not only do I want to emphasize that this is a must-read for business and technology leaders globally, I also want to echo his views—that it is in this current point in history that China is finally emerging as a global player in technology.

Over the past few decades, China's technological, and perhaps even industrial, development has been driven by models from the West. Having been the CTO of Tencent—now the world's fourth largest Internet company by revenue (2015)—for eight years, I have witnessed many changes in the market. In the early days we were not immune to the temptation of simple adaption from the West. At that point in time, speed was essential to establishing one's foothold in the market, and many companies favored "copying" over "creating." However, the last few years in China have seen a dramatic change in how products are developed. As our country's corporations have matured, we have begun to look deeper at consumer needs, and have become adept at evolving existing business and technological models into new models that look nothing like their Western counterparts.

At Tencent, our QQ instant messaging service had long held the largest share of the instant messaging market. So, when we decided to launch WeChat in 2011, we decided to create something resolutely Chinese. We did this by building our design upon the unique social habits of Chinese users, which were primarily based on intimate social circles. Because of this insight into Chinese consumers, we managed to build WeChat into the largest mobile communication tool in China in a couple of years. Globally, it is now used by over 600 million users in many countries. In China, WeChat is used not only for interpersonal needs, but also as the de facto communication tool for doing business.

But why stop at a communication tool? WeChat strengthened its foothold by helping people to connect the digital world with the physical. It has become a platform for users to access all their lifestyle needs, allowing them to communicate with smart devices, purchase offline services and goods, send digital payments, and interact with companies and brands. But WeChat's current shift into a lifestyle platform is just one beacon of the emerging online-to-offline (O2O) and IoT revolution in China.

About one year ago, I departed from Tencent to launch my new fund, Seven Seas Ventures. The fund's mission and belief are that China's rapid and pervasive diffusion of technology (most notably its astounding smartphone penetration) over the past years will make China one of the most important growth beds for IoT in the next decade. This is why we are actively investing in high-tech startups with the potential for global technological disruption.

There are certain times in history where the cards of nations are shuffled significantly. Living in these times, we can sense that things are rapidly changing, possibilities flashing before us, but with no obvious landing point. Yet, at the same time, we know that when things settle down, the landscape of the world will look significantly different. At these turning points, attempts at making firm predictions are often difficult. However, in his book, Marco, armed with the collective knowledge of the leaders of China's tech industry, has allowed us a rare glimpse into how China will shape the global technological model, not only for the year to come, but also for the next decade. Certainly, I hope to play a role in this change, and I hope that this book may also inspire you too.

Jeff Xiong
Founder of Seven Seas Ventures
Former CTO of Tencent

Preface

What would you do when you suddenly have an intuition? A gut feeling about something not visible yet, but that still makes sense to you. Normally you could have two reactions. You acknowledge your feeling, but you do not act upon it, or you'd try to see it through. I chose the second way.

When I sat down to write East-Commerce in 2014 I intended to tell the story of a quest and raise a very provocative question *What if China has developed a technological model so advanced that eventually will spread around the world?*

As chapters piled up, it dawned on me, back then, that publishers might dismiss my theory as premature. Alibaba was certainly making news, but a new technological model seemed like a far stretch. "Is there a story to tell?" They would ask me each time I pitched my book. When I approached the end of my writing I asked myself whether I had arrived at the stadium too early for the game. An *East-Commerce* was not evident yet, but I could not wait for publishers to acknowledge it. This is when I discovered Amazon self-publishing tool. By basically uploading my word files, in just a few hours, I could be visible on The Everything Store in the Kindle section. And this is how I proceeded.

When the e-book came out, I was not sure what would happen next. I had finally put, in black and white, the summary of a very long search where I interviewed over 200 people including more than 20 CEOs throughout 4 continents. So I decided to make a little experiment. I printed the book and went on a roadshow to present it at various conferences. This is when things started to get interesting.

As word came out that the first book on China e-commerce had been written, people were immediately interested for the most disparate reasons. It is always fascinating to see how differently individuals can use the same piece of information. Investors reached out for insights on who would be the best horses to bet on. International businesses contacted me to learn more about the innovative business models described in my book. Finally, Chinese companies asked me where East-Commerce is heading *Will it take over America and Europe too?* From what I was seeing, I had arrived at the stadium at the right time!

Meanwhile, something else was happening. The powerful technological forces detailed in my book certainly did not stop when it first came out. On each leg of my roadshow, people wanted to know more. To answer their questions I constantly monitored Chinese e-commerce developments. I also came in touch with many more companies, Chinese and International, and spent a great deal of time understanding how they operate. Hence, I was inevitably already updating the book in my mind. This is why I decided, together with my newly acquired publisher, that writing an updated and expanded version of *East-Commerce* would make a great deal of sense.

In this new edition I have expanded several sections. For example, O2O (online-to-offline) has seen an incredible explosion in 2015 and talking to Baidu, at the forefront of this sector, gave me a privileged access to what is happening. This is when I have learnt that O2O is pushing a macro shift in the economy between a consumption-based growth in favor of services lead growth. In fact, services in 2015 have accounted for more than 50% of China's GDP.

Getting in touch with retail companies and new e-commerce platforms helped me craft a new chapter on how a well-known fashion brand has conquered China's e-commerce market. But this is not all. Something quite unique is happening. Until 2014 BAT-X, China's biggest platforms, were competing against each other in many different services from group buying to taxi hailing apps. Lately, we are seeing platforms striking alliances among themselves. They are starting to realize that peace and cooperation bring better results when exploring unchartered territories.

East-Commerce is also going full steam. Chinese Internet and e-commerce platforms are now investing abroad at a growing speed. In the Indian market, Alibaba has made important moves, successfully replicating its Chinese model. In the African market, Tencent is making a great leap forward so as Baidu and Xiaomi in other emerging economies. The intuition, the gut feeling, is now fully visible.

But there is an important issue I shall address here. In this book I will often mention that while some things are constantly evolving in China, others remain unchanged. Since the technology world moves at an exponential speed, the companies mentioned here will inevitably evolve, consolidate or even disappear. While I follow these changes in my blog, the scope of this book isn't to be up to date on who's who and what they are up to. It is not either to predict which companies will come out ahead and which will wind down in flames. It is to explain the underlying principles behind e-commerce and the Internet of Things. The trends and dynamics described here will need at least a few more years to come to full maturity.

This brings me to address a pressing question that relentlessly concerns investors and markets *Is China's e-commerce massive growth sustainable?* In other words *What happens if the economy stops growing?* When looking closely at what is happening, we can see that nothing has really changed. The underlying consumption growth is still there. But this is not actually the point.

I will elaborate my answer. China has been a key source of growth for international companies for decades, but in 2015 GDP's growth has slowed to a figure deemed to be somewhere between 5 and 7%. The share price of some of China's e-commerce and Internet platforms has decreased in value – sometime even considerably. Hence the world is questioning China's future. According to a study from a well-known Think Tank, The Demand Institute, and Nielsen – Sold in China – in the next decade China's GDP growth will slow even more. Why is it so? China is trying to shift from an economy dependent on export and investments toward domestic consumption. Chinese economy appears to look more and more like a two-headed dragon. One side is slowing down – export and investments – while another – the tertiary sector – is still growing. Anyhow, whether or not China makes this transition, The Demand Institute predicts that consumption might still grow up to 60% in 10 years. So consumption remains strong.

What role do Internet and e-commerce play in this growth? They are the underlying force behind a new class of consumers: the "connected consumers". Violette, the main character of this book, is a clear example. According to another report from The Demand Institute – No more Tiers – by 2025 the connected consumers will account for 80% of growth in consumption and connectivity will almost single handedly sustain their growth, giving them access to information and retail channels.

This is why, in my opinion, Internet and e-commerce are so important in China despite how much the GDP will grow. They have become part of this new consumers' culture, enhancing their life through virtualization and have brought an irreversible change. Those who get caught up in measuring China's technological revolution by purely looking at shares prices or statistics – instead of as phenomenon that has brought a massive shift in the society and business – are missing the global impact of this change.

Eventually I will stop updating this book, but for the moment I am just enjoying the chance to keep sharing my findings.

Marco Gervasi
Shanghai
February 2016

Acknowledgments

They say that writing a book is like becoming a parent. At the beginning your child takes everything out of you, and later it gives it back to you piece by piece. Though that sounds a bit extreme and somewhat limiting, I tend to agree with this, at least in terms of writing a book. At the beginning of this project I told myself that I could finish the very first book on China e-commerce in just four months. I simply wanted to write a small guide. My estimate was ambitious, and, as I discovered, unrealistic; days turned into weeks, which eventually turned into a 12-month marathon.

In many ways writing a book is also like launching a startup. Plans never go quite as predicted. But I like to think that it is often for the best.

Both a child and a startup need hard work and support. And in both cases, the outcome is a mix of its DNA, or of an idea, and the environment where the idea grows.

Looking back, I realize that the original idea of this book had been developing over the course of many years, with experiences gathered from around the world. Most of its genes were sort of free floating in my notepads—where, once in a while, I would write down comments, opinions, sketches and most of all events and meetings that inspired me—before the process of arranging them in this book and weaving a story even got started.

It took me a while to find the right team to transform my ideas and stories into the structure of this book. The small guide that I had originally intended turned into a manual, which eventually turned into a tale. I went through a series of trials and errors, and the beauty of it was that my ideas were enriched by the people that I met along my journey. Their suggestions and points of view made my child grow up stronger and more aware of the world it was living in.

I begin these acknowledgment pages with Jennifer Johnson. She helped me in the very challenging task, so far one of the most challenging, of patiently weaving my stories until they turned into this book. I will always be grateful for the uncountable number of hours she dedicated to discussing ideas, editing my drafts and giving me suggestions.

I owe a huge debt to another friend, Toby Overmaat, who was frank enough to tell me, four months into the writing process, that my book was full of information, but it was bereft of a story. Being a lawyer, I thought that I knew how to write, but I could not have been more wrong. Toby has been a strong supporter, providing outstanding advice to craft the book's outline, helping me explain what East-Commerce really means and creating the three pillars. She has watched the book like a mentor, providing great support and stepping in whenever necessary.

I am indebted to the people whose experiences form the backbone of this book: Porter Erisman, Jacky Xue, Fan Fan, Bruce Nikoo, William Tanuwijaya, Jeffrey Kang, Junling Liu, Toine Rooijmans, Onno Schreurs, Dexter Lu, Kunal Bahl, Thibault Villet, JP Gan, Violette Kong, and everyone who has contributed by sharing their experience. I am grateful to have been able to recruit these extraordinary people as characters—and even more grateful for the opportunity to have learned from them in the process.

In conducting the research necessary to understand what e-commerce really is and how it works, a special thanks goes to Edoardo Carfagna, who was my research analyst and traveling mate for the first leg of my journey through China e-commerce. He brought the spirit and the critical voice of the younger generation into analyzing the impact of mobile on e-commerce, something I had initially underestimated. I also thank him for suggesting *East-Commerce* as the title for this book.

I am indebted to Enrico Mattoli, Erica Poon Werkun, and many of their colleagues at UBS Hong Kong, for their continuous support and the opportunity to present my books and ideas to their unique audience. And finally, for granting me access to some of the most inspiring leaders in the world of Asian e-commerce.

A special thanks goes also to Jeffrey Kang and Feng Li from Cogobuy for introducing me to the fascinating world of the Internet of Things. I could have not written this very important part of the book if they hadn't been willing to spend time talking with me. A special thanks goes also to Alessandro Duina and to Prodygia.com for helping me transform this project into an online education tool and for supporting me with my bold plans. I have finally found my "bone to chew".

Finally, I would like to thank Jeff Xiong for accepting to write the foreword to this book and for showing me that technology has no more borders.

Like a father looking at his son on the day he turns 18, there were times when joy and sorrow alternated, when he gave me doubts and worries that kept me awake, but I never questioned the pride I felt as he was growing up. He is now free to live in the world and make it more special.

This is how I see my book and my journey so far.

About the Author

Marco Gervasi is the founder and managing director of The Red Synergy where he provides management consulting assistance to leading international and Chinese companies, venture capital funds, and Internet platforms investing both in and out of China. He also advises leading Chinese companies on how to become exponential organizations. He has over twelve years of senior corporate management experience in China and is one of the world's leading experts on China e-commerce and IOT. He is a keynote speaker at international conferences on technology, a guest writer for various newspapers and magazines both in Asia and Europe, and an active technology blogger www.marcogervasiwrites.com. He lives in Shanghai.

The East-Commerce Video Course

My goal is that this book is not the end of the conversation, but the beginning.

Together with the education site Prodygia (www.prodygia.com) I have prepared a 60-minute video course on China e-commerce (Your Introductory Course on E-Commerce in China And Why It Matters To Your Business) that you can find at http://prodygia.com/courses/23-your-introductory-course-on-e-commerce-in-china-and-why-it-matters-to-your-business. Here you can explore topics critical to China e-commerce—from understanding China's unique e-commerce model, to starting an e-commerce business in China. Book readers will be entitled to a 50 percent discount on the course using the promo code: ecomm1.

I also invite you to continue the discussion with me on the developments of China e-commerce and the Internet of Things by following the book's website: http://www.east-commerce.com. Here you will find my blog (A Quote on Singularities) where I will update readers weekly on the latest news on technology from around the world.

Finally, you can reach me at marco.gervasi@east-commerce.com.

Illustration Credit

The illustrations in this book were drawn by Shelby Chen on an iPhone. Shelby began to draw finger sketches on his first iPhone in 2011 to capture snippets of his life. These small pieces of digital art take 20–30 minutes to sketch and are often posted on social media and also featured in the Financial Times Chinese website in 2013. Shelby also dedicates part of his time to *Wings of Music*, a children's charity program he helped create as a founding trustee in 2009, teaching underprivileged children classical music (www.wingsofmusic.org).

Shelby was born and raised in Beijing and worked in the U.S. during the 90s. He is a managing partner of a leading Chinese venture capital firm focused on investing in environment technology companies. His work takes him around China and the world.

He lives in Beijing with his wife, Jeane, and daughter, Claire.

His email is: chenshelby@gmail.com

CHAPTER 1

The Great (Technological) Leap Forward

Shelby 2013.9.21

Kong Wei—or Violette, as she much prefers—puts on her black jacket, switches off her computer and powers down her office ready to leave. It's a Wednesday in May, one of Violette's favorite months; it is the start of the rainy season that nourishes crops, so meaningful even here in the heart of Shanghai's Xin Tian Di business district.

At 37, Violette is a veteran merchandiser who, like many ambitious Chinese, has worked her way up the ladder. She began her career

1

overseeing quality control, enforcing international companies' production standards with visits to factories across China. Soon she was responsible for producing collections from sports to fashion at several European and U.S. apparel companies. Her most recent promotion made her the head of merchandising and e-commerce for an American entertainment corporation. With her trendy haircut, silver shoes and stylish white handbag, Violette's style is very Stella McCartney.

Violette's office building, by a manmade lake, has the best view of the area. McKinsey's China headquarters stands across the street. As she quickly descends to the now-deserted lobby, Violette reflects on the contrast between her work now and back during those brutally cold and horribly hot days inspecting rural factories. She has earned her corner office the hard way.

The story of Violette's journey is, in many ways, the same as China's. Xin Tian Di was once a historic district with hundreds of two-story lane houses—the so-called *Shikumen* built around a tiny central court. Originally single-family homes, they were converted to communal use during the Cultural Revolution. Several years ago, a well-known developer from Hong Kong bought the entire area and recreated the lane house spirit, but with a modern twist. The district is now populated with international galleries, bars and cafes, boutiques and theme restaurants. You might see a 20-something woman parking the latest McLaren or Maserati in front of the First Congress Hall of the Communist Party of China and not think twice.

As Violette leaves the office, she worries that the rain may have dispersed the line of taxis that normally wait in front of her building. She could take the underground home, but it is raining. Since it is now 8:30 p.m., her company will reimburse her 40-minute cab ride to the Minhang District in the outskirts of Shanghai. She reaches into her bag, grabs her phone, opens the taxi section of WeChat and books a ride. Tonight she is lucky: she just needs to tip her driver, who is already waiting at the entrance, a very small amount to agree to pick her up.

Shanghai may be ultra-modern, but its cabs are a throwback to the past. Violette's ride is in an old Volkswagen with no dashboard navigation system. She asks if her driver knows her destination. He taps the maps application of Baidu, China's Google equivalent, on his smartphone; soon a voice is ready to guide him through the city to deliver Violette home. Old infrastructures, new remedies.

Violette uses the 40-minute ride to run some virtual errands. Her new assistant, Wang Wang, has been working hard, as their team expanded from two to nine staffers in just a few months to prepare for the launch of the company's first e-commerce store. They recruited an e-commerce team, hired a digital marketing agency and built a customer relationship center. It has been pretty hectic.

Remembering Wang Wang's sweet tooth, Violette opens the Groupon-like gift card application Kaado, purchases a portion of green tea tiramisu cake and sends the e-voucher to Wang Wang. The gift card is a promotion for customers paying with Alipay, Alibaba's version of PayPal. Tomorrow morning, Wang Wang will be able to stop by the bakery on her way into work, show the code on her phone and pick up the cake.

Violette is finally home. She thanks the driver and gets out of her cab. The fare has already been paid via the taxi application.

The Journey

Violette's story is an example of how convenient life has become for many people in China, even more so than in the West. This was made possible by the changes brought about by technology. I discovered the extent of these changes during a two-year journey that took me back and forth between China and Silicon Valley, and these two places became the setting for this story.

But how did it all start? I first set foot in China in 1996, when I went to study Mandarin at Fudan University in Shanghai for two summer terms. Back then, the Internet was just an exotic tool only accessible to the few and mainly at Internet cafes. To write emails and keep in touch with family and friends, I had to walk 20 minutes to reach the nearest cafe. Sometimes, I had to stand in line for up to one hour to use one of the few Lenovo PCs available. The connection was poor and Web pages loaded slowly. In the mid-1990s it seemed pretty hard to envision that one day people in China would live like Violette.

At the beginning of the new millennium, after graduating from university in Italy, I joined a law firm in Milan and worked for four years as a securities lawyer. During the dotcom boom and bust years I was part of the firm's capital markets team helping, among others, tech companies get listed both in Italy and in the U.S.

According to Alexa, a well-respected company providing commercial Web traffic information now owned by Amazon, the Internet was still a very Western thing in the early 2000s. In September 2000, excluding Japan and Korea, the first ten Internet companies in terms of traffic were all American. The Internet was indeed a tool for the developed world.[1]

In 2004, I made the move to Shanghai where I initially worked for a local business and management consulting company. Then, in 2007, I became an entrepreneur, founding an advisory firm to help foreign businesses set up new ventures or partner with local businesses in China.

Those were the years of China's massive industrialization and double-digit growth. China saw its biggest boom after joining the World Trade Organization in 2001, building infrastructures like cities, ports, airports and industrial zones. From multinationals to small and medium companies, everyone was setting up operations in China. It felt like unless a company was there, it would not be able to compete on a global scale.

It was business as usual until 2012, when I traveled to visit a friend in San Francisco. There, I became fascinated by the energy and perpetual pursuit of innovation in the U.S. tech industry.

I sensed that Silicon Valley and China were somehow on a collision course, but I was not sure how they would intersect. They could not be more different. China was focused on manual labor and heavy industry. Silicon Valley was driven by technology and efficiency. Gut feelings are often hard to explain.

Inspired by what I saw in the Bay Area, when I returned to China, I decided to hold a round of interviews and ask my clients—and their clients—what they believed the future held for their businesses. How were they innovating?

It was then that I realized that China and its market were on the brink of major change. In over 30 interviews, one concept kept recurring: *Offices will be the factories of the future.* I learned that companies were automating to become more efficient, as factories cut their workforce. Machines were simply cheaper and did not go on strike.

Automation caused labor-related costs to decline globally, so multinationals began to consolidate production back home, closer to their customers. China was about to say goodbye to a lot of traditional industrial businesses. Meanwhile, technology was lowering entry barriers, allowing many small, local players to compete with multinationals. They could now produce goods less expensively and in smaller batches. Huge factories with armies of workers were giving way to smaller, leaner and more efficient operations.

As competition increased, China was ceasing to be a profitable market for everyone. Margins eroded and technology became more important. China was no longer the place of cheap labor.

I kept on chewing on that phrase: *Offices will be the factories of the future.* What they were saying, I told myself, was that industrial businesses were giving way to more technological businesses. Technological? *Technological?* I mulled over that concept for a while before the realization hit me: *They are telling me technology might soon be China's new booming sector.*

But which technology, and in which way?

I didn't set out to become a specialist in technology. In school, I was more interested in the arts than the sciences. When I finally got a smartphone in 2007, I used it mainly for calls and messages, and seldom opened my browser.

In other words, I was like many people of my generation. But it was time for a change.

In 2013 I took a sabbatical and went traveling. I wanted to understand more about this change I was sensing. I felt that by staying in China, I was too close to the source to be able see the big picture. My rudimentary knowledge of traditional Chinese medicine taught me that when looking at a problem, the solution might come from a place where it is least expected.

It was during one of my trips that I bumped into an old friend in a coffee shop in Milan. He told me about a place in California called Singularity University. Based in Mountain View, the Internet's epicenter, and funded by, among others, NASA, Google, Cisco and Genentech, Singularity University helps people understand how to use advanced technologies with the potential to impact billions of people. It was a ten-day visit to the year 2033, a world where Google cars, 3D-printed body parts, flying drones and many other sci-fi objects were part of my daily life.

Classes were challenging and days were long, but it felt like I was finally getting my brain's upgrade. During breaks, I would stretch my legs with a walk along the military runway inside the campus. On one side I could see Motorola and Cisco's office buildings. On the other, the NASA laboratories, which developed many of the components of the Rover robot that was sent to Mars. I was in Silicon Valley, the cradle of innovation.

As I walked, my mind was drawn back to the East and to recurring questions about how technology would transform China in the years to come. I knew that China was searching for a sustainable way to provide a better life for its people—as expressed in the Shanghai 2010 Expo slogan: "Better City, Better Life."

I had yet to discover that a profound technological revolution was already under way in China. In California, while we were busy learning about the advent of a future period during which the technological change would irreversibly transform human life, the so-called Singularity, we were not talking about where it would happen first. It had not yet occurred to me that it might happen in China. At that point Mountain View seemed very far from Shanghai.

After Singularity, I set up a blog and began writing on tech-related matters. Technology became my passion. My focus was on how technology is touching our lives, the changes it is bringing and how to best take advantage of it.

A few months later, I was back in Shanghai. One afternoon, while waiting for a taxi in the prime area of West Nanjing Road, Shanghai's equivalent of Ginza in Tokyo or Park Avenue in New York, a client who was with me pointed to a brand new department store across the street and said, "Department stores might soon be in trouble. This whole Chinese e-commerce *thing* is giving them a hard time." To him, e-commerce was a mystery, a black box of sorts. My mind again returned to the idea of China and technology. Change was in the air, though I did not fully understand to what extent.

It all came together on November 11, 2013, China's Singles Day. Invented in 2009 by Alibaba, China's biggest e-commerce company, Singles Day is a marketing tool to boost online sales during the low season. Singles, by definition, do not have a partner to buy a present for. Therefore, they buy for themselves or for their friends.

The new holiday's date was chosen by numerology. The number one in Chinese refers to the unit as well as the state of being single. In Chinese, the number one is pronounced same as "I want." Two times the number one means that you really want something: "I want I want!" Four times the number one means that you are *very* determined to get what you want.

And those Chinese singles certainly were determined. In just 24 hours, Alibaba sold almost 5.8 billion USD of goods online, twice the American Cyber Monday online sales record. The best seller was Xiaomi, China's most famous smartphone.

Overnight, post offices were flooded with millions of packages— so many that it took logistics companies months to deliver them. When you have millions of people buying everything from shoes, to LCD screens, to electric scooters, delivery becomes quite a challenge. They do not fit into a standard mailbox. Entire sections of lobbies were designated as storage areas for November 11 deliveries. Elevators were jammed as people went up and down to sort their packages.

This is when I realized that, while I had been busy helping my clients set up factories and research centers, something huge had happened. China made another great leap forward, but this time it was a technological leap. I'd almost missed it. I had thought that the Internet and e-commerce were just tools to make my life more convenient. I was not very interested in understanding them beyond what I needed to for my daily tasks such as sending emails and drafting documents. But that was all about to change. They were no longer "just" tools; they had become two of China's biggest drivers. Suddenly, I found myself living in the same country, but in a different world. This technological leap was changing the rules of the game and it was something that I wanted to learn more about.

According to Alexa, as of October 2015, among the top ten Internet companies, two are now Chinese. Among the top 20, six are Chinese, one is Russian and one is Indian.[2] The Internet has become a critical tool for fast growing emerging market companies.

My mind returned to that military runway in Mountain View. At Singularity, our task was to come up with ideas that would impact 1 billion people. I realized that if you developed a "killer app" for China, at least based on what I was seeing, it would certainly impact 1 billion people. However, it seemed that very few people in the West were talking about the effect that technology was already having on this massive Chinese market.

I knew that hundreds of millions of people like Violette were using applications like Baidu's maps, social networks like WeChat, taxi applications like Didi Dache and mobile payment systems like Alipay or TenPay. They were using them in ways that I had never seen before, not even on Google's campus.

The very same technology that originated in the Bay Area was already in China, but it was being used in a very unique way. Inspired by many applications developed in Silicon Valley, Chinese applications have been adapted for Chinese consumers who are much more digitally sophisticated than Western consumers. While I was busy using Excel and PowerPoint to draft documents and presentations on my laptop, young Chinese were embracing their mobiles without ever having owned a PC.

I felt I was picking up on something that others in the West had not yet noticed, and I wanted to share what I was seeing. China had gone through a technological revolution with e-commerce being its headlight. But writing a few articles or blog posts is far from embarking on research for a book on such a complex topic. Over drinks with a tech writer one evening in Milan in early 2014, I described my idea as well as my concerns.

My writer friend listened to me and replied, "You spent ten years in China helping companies start up their businesses. During this time you witnessed tremendous changes. You are now talking about a new important change, a China 3.0. Don't you think that this phenomenon might have an impact even outside China? Maybe even here, 9,000 kilometers from the epicenter?" In other words: *What are you waiting for?* And there I was, 7 p.m. on a January evening in Milan. I dropped everything I was doing. A few days later, I was back in China to begin my research.

A Brief History of China E-Commerce

The first two questions I wanted to answer were: *How did e-commerce begin its ascent in China?* and *Why has it become so important?* E-commerce is in fact not just a commercial tool in China. It has become a model for economic development.

According to a McKinsey Global Institute report, China's growth model has shifted from one centered around production and export, to a new model driven by the Internet and technology.[3] In particular, the report noted: "The heavy capital investment and labor force expansion that fueled China's rise over the past two decades cannot be sustained indefinitely." What this means is that, enabled by the Internet, China has migrated to a new economy based on productivity, innovation and domestic consumption. E-commerce is moving China from a "2.0" to a much more efficient "China 3.0" model. This is why e-commerce has become so important. It is not just a new way to do something old—such as selling goods and services through the Internet; it is now a driver of growth.

But how did it all start? At the end of the last century, America's emerging e-commerce model fascinated China, whose commercial infrastructure was very underdeveloped. With its vast territory and huge population, it would cost too much and take too long to bring department stores and modern shops to every major city in China. E-commerce could reach those far-flung locations faster than bricks-and-mortar shops.

However, China could not simply adopt the U.S. model, which had been designed for a developed market and built on top of the traditional retail infrastructure. Mom-and-pop businesses, not American-style large national retailers such as Walmart and Macy's, were still the backbone of Chinese commerce.

Serving customers across China using an Amazon-like system would have been cost prohibitive: Amazon owns most of the inventory it sells, and has poured millions into sourcing and distribution. To generate Amazon's economies of scale, Chinese Internet companies would need to internalize functions like warehousing and logistics, and hire millions of people.

Can you imagine a company with 20 million employees? The entire population of the Netherlands would not be enough. Not exactly a viable option.

The model had to be adapted to Chinese specifications. The first, and to date the most successful, Chinese digital platform, Alibaba, found that the best way for an e-commerce business to succeed was not by recreating Amazon, but by building an eBay-like platform connecting buyers and sellers, leaving to others the costly business of moving goods.

In 2003, Taobao, China's most iconic e-commerce platform, was initially structured as an enabler connecting buyers to sellers. This ingenious shift from an Amazon model to an eBay model for micro businesses caused Chinese e-commerce to take off despite its undeveloped bricks-and-mortar infrastructure.

China E-Commerce Model in a Nutshell

Passion, energy and curiosity prompted me to embark on a journey to define this mysterious "thing" (as my client had referred to it) called Chinese e-commerce and discover how it works.

China e-commerce is based on three characteristics or pillars: it fosters bottom-up growth, it has created a super connected world and it is extremely social. It is also significantly more advanced than Western e-commerce because it is designed with smartphones in mind, and scaled to a market of hundreds of millions.

The first pillar of China e-commerce is the empowerment of young people and rural area inhabitants. Becoming an entrepreneur and pursuing a better life in China is now easier than it ever has been before. Anyone can now set up an online store and sell products without needing to own a production site. Platforms like Alibaba's Taobao and Tmall are enabling millions of individuals to become online entrepreneurs, also known as "Taobao Sellers." Suddenly, running a "Taobao Shop" has become a real job for millions of young Chinese people.

Entrepreneurship is not just confined to urban areas. It has spread to rural towns, the so-called Taobao Villages, where the capacity to set up an online shop offers people an alternative to leaving home in search of work at a faraway factory or construction site. In essence, e-commerce platforms have democratized national entrepreneurship and promoted development throughout China. This has ignited a new kind of expansion: a bottom-up growth.

This concept of bottom-up growth is key to understanding a new breed of Chinese entrepreneurs. Traditionally, growth in China has been extremely centralized, or top-down. The central economy planned certain things and made them happen. Infrastructures like highways, high-speed railways, urbanization and IT grids have been the drivers of economic growth, mainly reserved for state-owned enterprises or joint ventures with major foreign partners.

Lately, however, private companies have been powering China's growth. Bottom-up startups and e-commerce platforms now enable entrepreneurs to create new products and services, bringing progress to industries. For the first time, a new group, the Chinese entrepreneurs and small and medium businesses, are empowered by e-commerce to have national impact.

The second pillar of China e-commerce is the creation of a super connected world. Thanks to the rapid mass diffusion of smart devices, China's online and offline worlds are now coming together in a revolutionary way that Mao never envisioned.

This is happening due to the lack of traditional infrastructure, which ultimately turned into China's biggest opportunity. To grow and prosper, e-commerce platforms and Internet companies have created an entirely new online infrastructure to support transactions. This structure is like an ecosystem, made up of online payments, smart logistics, and customer service applications. This ecosystem has connected the physical and the virtual worlds in a way that has not yet happened in the West. Chinese e-commerce has become so efficient that people use it even in their "offline" life. For example, the concept of a seamless experience, or "click and pick" where you buy something online and pick it up offline, has been refined into a science in China. While "O2O" (online to offline) sounds futuristic in the West, it is already part of China's present.

Finally, Chinese e-commerce has turned shopping into a social experience, which is the third pillar. Chinese people love to chat, exchange opinions on products, share pictures and give feedback. Commerce and social are now converging. WeChat, a mobile-only social application and media platform with more that 600 million users,[4] is not only a messaging application, but also a mobile news reading application, blogging platform, online storefront and mobile wallet—all in one. The more Chinese people buy, the more it becomes a social experience.

The three pillars combined have given rise to an e-commerce model that has become fully integrated and where online shopping, chatting and booking are remarkably advanced. This model is now being closely watched and even imitated by the developed world. Meanwhile, in the other parts of the developing world, with underdeveloped infrastructures similar to China, this model is being fully embraced. From Indonesia to Nigeria, it is becoming more and more common to hear that the Chinese e-commerce "way" suits their developing economies better than the "everything store way" prevalent in the West.

Despite Western assumptions, Silicon Valley's Internet and e-commerce startups are no longer the sole source of business-model disruption, or even the most important. For the first time, they are about to be challenged by a new non-Western model.

Chinese e-commerce is a new commercial and growth model that is conquering the East and becoming a source of inspiration for Asia and potentially the rest of the world. That is why I have named it: *East-Commerce.*

Where It Is Heading

When looking at the rapid growth of China e-commerce, I could not initially understand how it could become so big so quickly or where it was going.

To answer these questions I reverted to one of the first teachings at Singularity University, about linear growth versus exponential growth. Let me elaborate this concept. For the majority of us, change occurs at the same rate that we have experienced it most recently. People intuitively assume that the current rate of progress will continue for future periods. For example, in the U.S., mass adoption of the radio took 31 years from its invention in 1897. When thinking about the Web, which was introduced in 1991, one might expect the same. Yet it took only seven years.[5]

How could that happen? The reason is that technology's growth isn't linear, but exponential. Long-range forecasts often drastically underestimate future developments because they are based on an "intuitive linear" approach rather than an exponential one.

Another example can be seen with the Internet penetration of Thailand. According to a UBS report: "Until end of 2012, Thailand was one of three countries in the world without 3G, alongside North Korea and Cuba. Now, Thailand has reached a level of Internet penetration, one year after the introduction of 3G services, that took China three and a half years to achieve."[6] Bottom line, when the growth is exponential things will happen much faster than we expect.

The difference between linear growth and exponential growth is the basis of how technology evolves. Exponential growth is based on the famous dictum called Moore's law, named for Intel co-founder Gordon E. Moore, who described the trend in a 1965 paper. Moore's law observes that the number of transistors on integrated circuits doubles approximately every two years. So every two years, integrated circuits become twice as powerful. In other words, the power of your computer or mobile phone doubles every two years.

Processing speed, memory capacity, sensors and even the number and size of pixels in digital cameras are strongly linked to Moore's law. Each of these is also improving at an exponential rate, which is why it took the Web only seven years to reach mass adoption while it took the radio thirty one, and also why Internet penetration is happening faster in Thailand than in China.

This explains why China e-commerce is growing faster than anywhere else, but to understand where it is heading we first need to look back at how this world of the Internet evolved.

In his award-winning book *The World is Flat*, Thomas Friedman described the personal computer as the change agent enabling anyone in the connected world to join the Internet and in turn create a unified world. That was 2005.

The wide diffusion of PCs and of the Internet made geography irrelevant and suddenly everyone became connected. This is when a new world started to unfold. This time it was not made of atoms, instead it was made of bits. It was the virtual world where millions of connected people started living in a new world of messages, chat and online communities.

However, while the world was becoming flat and virtual thanks to the PCs produced by China, China was still lagging behind. In fact, being an export-driven economy, it was not buying most of the PCs it was manufacturing, as the majority were designated for export.

The real technological revolution arrived in China thanks to another device: the smartphone. This was the agent that enabled mass connectivity and became the tool to access the Internet and the virtual world.

In fact, while PC makers were busy working on more powerful semiconductors, mobile phone developers fully benefited from Moore's law and engineered, in a much shorter time than it took to develop PCs' integrated circuits, phones powerful enough to replace PCs. When faced with the choice between a PC, a laptop or a mobile phone, Chinese consumers went straight to mobile, bypassing laptops and PCs completely. They were smaller, more powerful—and cheaper.

Thanks to this vast diffusion of smartphones, the Chinese are now moving one step past the rest of the world in creating a super connected world where the physical and virtual dimensions meet inside a mobile phone in the most seamless of ways.

Violette is a good example. During her taxi ride, she effortlessly steps into one world and comes out into another: purchasing a cake online for offline pickup, or browsing clothes online, trying them in a shop, and then purchasing them on a website. E-commerce has made this possible because its platforms have connected the two worlds.

What does this mean for the future? This super connected world will create new efficient business models. In sectors such as retail, automotive, finance, healthcare and many others, these models will connect the physical and the virtual worlds.

This efficiency will be driven by both the Internet and hardware. The world is on the brink of full adoption of wearables such as Google Glass, the iWatch, Oculus Rift and Avegant's Glyph, devices that signal the advent of the Internet of Things. They have even more potential to connect the Chinese than mobile phones. A billion Chinese, connected to billions of devices, will begin to live an "extraterrestrial" life, interacting continuously and moving between the physical and virtual worlds. With the Internet of Things, Chinese e-commerce will grow even bigger thanks to a mountain of data transmitted by these devices.

Understanding how e-commerce works, and how to benefit from it, means more than simply learning how to sell something online in China. Eventually all of us will change our habits and learn to live between the physical and virtual worlds. Chinese e-commerce offers a glimpse into the future and shows us what this new, seamless world might soon look like.

The Internet, e-commerce and social networks are products of the West, yet Chinese innovation is allowing a mass diffusion of these technologies on a huge scale. So far, everyone is still looking to the West, thinking that innovation comes only in one form: inventing something unique, which becomes revolutionary. However, something that at first might seem paradoxical is happening in China. The innovation brought about by China, an incremental innovation on a mass scale, is changing the emerging world and will soon influence the developed world as well. This will be a new type of revolution, one that is brought about by evolution.

2

A Perfect Blend

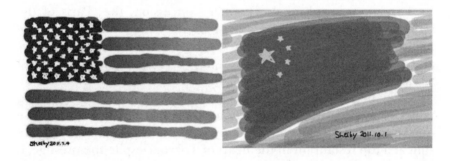

The bustling streets of the French Concession district are still thronged with a mix of tourists and Shanghai's professional set as Jacky Xue walks his last customers to the door. A light summer breeze brushes the young restaurateur as he crosses the main room. It has been a big night for his restaurant, Primo, Jacky's newest Italian fine dining offering, which, after a difficult start, has suddenly become "the" spot for Shanghai's foodies and scenesters.

Jacky removes his jacket, inscribed with his name in English and Chinese, *Xue Zhe Jun,* and drapes it over a dark leather sofa by the wine cellar. His look is refined: 32, and stylishly dressed, he cuts a slim figure for a chef. He deliberately affects the look of Western-style celebrity chefs often seen advertising gourmet food.

Walking past the open kitchen, Jacky slides into a seat at a corner table by a brick wall graced by newly hung works from an up-and-coming German photographer. Nearby is a photo of the chef with two Chinese models. The restaurant's look is just what Jacky had envisioned: neat and elegant, like a trendy Tokyo restaurant. He notices a recently delivered parcel on the table, a present from a loyal customer. It is a wooden box containing fine green tea from Fujian, a region in southeast China renowned for its teas. His assistant sees him, and comes over to discuss the coming week's menu.

The French Concession district owes its name to the 1842 Treaty of Nanjing, in which foreign nations were granted settlements and concessions in Shanghai. The first French consul, who arrived in early 1848 to look after the interests of his community, negotiated a 66-hectare area bounded by the Huangpu River to the east and the much larger British Concession to the north.

Foreigners speak of the French Concession, the "Paris of the Orient," as a little piece of home in an otherwise exotic city. Shanghainese will tell you that it is quiet, protected by a long line of trees and populated with boutiques and cafes—it is one of Shanghai's most vibrant places.

Jacky began his long journey to the French Concession waiting tables to pay his way through hotel school in Shanghai, and rose quickly through the kitchen's hierarchy. Graduation was followed by a stint at a top restaurant in the heart of Tokyo. Despite the prestige, it was neither an easy nor glamorous period, and not speaking Japanese was quite a disadvantage.

Jacky did not choose Japan at random. His goal was to master the art of cooking and bring something special back to China. He started with a plum assignment in one of Tokyo's most famous Italian restaurants where he spent the first six months learning to use the kitchen's knives to cut vegetables—he was not yet allowed to cook. Within two years he had become a key member of the team and had finally learned to speak Japanese as well as Italian. More importantly, he learned the patience of Japanese chefs, their endless search for perfection and impeccable service.

At age 28, Jacky left Tokyo for Milan, to work as an aid to a chef at a Michelin two-star restaurant. He learned to master signature dishes like the yellow saffron rice called *Risotto alla Milanese*. There, he set a new goal for himself: to win the coveted three-star rating from Michelin.

So, Jacky returned to Shanghai and opened two Italian restaurants: Top Chef and then Primo. The names symbolize his dream of being the best at what he does and the goal of joining Michelin's Olympus.

Chinese E-Commerce Is Unique

One night in Shanghai several months ago, a friend suggested dinner at Jacky's Primo, then newly opened. As an Italian, I'm generally not a fan of eating Italian food abroad; I prefer to eat the local cuisine especially when it is as delicious as that of Shanghai. My friend insisted. He wondered whether I'd find Primo's food authentic. And so we went.

International restaurants in China cater mainly to a foreign crowd—their cuisine is often too foreign for Chinese tastes. But to our surprise, we were the only non-Chinese customers at Primo that night. Noticing that the restaurant was filled with locals, we decided to approach Jacky and ask him a few questions. We were curious to know his secret. A bottle of Limoncello in hand, he joined us at our table.

We asked Jacky how he made foreign food so successful among locals while holding to Milanese standards. After pouring us a drink, he told us his story. His secret was simple: patience and trust.

As we warmed to the conversation (and the Limoncello), Jacky explained the details of his winning strategy. To differentiate himself from hundreds of Chinese chefs, he opened an Italian restaurant. He took advantage of his international training to generate curiosity. Then he started educating his customers.

To build trust, Jacky began with basic dishes: a simple salad with an olive oil and vinegar dressing. He then introduced diners to meat, fish, truffles, oysters, fine wine and desserts. Chinese people are very curious and love to try new things. Though attracted to foreign things, they need time to develop an appreciation for something that is new to them.

Whenever new customers, local or foreign, came into his restaurants, Jacky would come out from the kitchen to help them order, explaining the menu in detail and learning their tastes.

From his kitchen, Jacky would watch his customers carefully. If a dish was half eaten, he would go over to the table and ask for feedback. If the customer did not like the dish, Jacky would remake it, free of charge, even if it meant altering the preparation drastically to suit their taste. The goal was to make his customers happy.

This strategy paid off. As he adapted the foreign flavors to local taste, altering as much as he needed to win acceptance, his customers eventually stopped looking at the menu and began trusting Jacky's recommendations.

Jacky played with his car keys as he told us how he managed to make *Risotto alla Milanese* even tastier for his Chinese customers: by topping it with a tiger prawn. Rice-based risotto is a main course in Milan, but in China it's a side dish. Adding a lone tiger prawn changed everything. It became so popular that everybody was ordering *Risotto alla Milanese.*

I thought to myself: "If you kept everything in this restaurant the same and simply replaced Jacky with an Italian chef, like a cut-and-paste, the restaurant would eventually close."

Foreign chefs who have been unsuccessful in China have long blamed the Chinese palate. They faulted the customer for not appreciating the nuances of Western cuisine. The Chinese mix wine with cool drinks; they prefer overcooked noodles to the *al dente* pasta so famous in Milan, Paris and New York. Foreign chefs often concluded that Chinese were unsophisticated and unable to fully appreciate the cuisines of the West.

Rarely in China have I seen a foreign chef come out of the kitchen to take a new customer's order. These chefs rarely put themselves on their customers' level, the way Jacky did.

No one else was willing to lose money and adapt recipes in order to educate and build clientele. But Jacky was. "China requires patience, lots of it," he preached.

Jacky's story is a bit like China's e-commerce story: the Chinese have taken something established in the West, adapted and iterated it in continuous cycles until arriving at something different—a unique blend suited to the Chinese taste.

No matter how obvious that sounds, it is this exact principal that many foreign businesses in China fail to accept. Foreign companies expect to make money from the very beginning and are unwilling to adapt the model that made them so successful in the first place. It may not be easy, but in China it is essential.

Taobao, eBay and the *Risotto Alla Milanese*

Founded in 1999, the Hangzhou-based Alibaba, China's biggest Internet company, is the spark that set fire to China's e-commerce. E-commerce really gained momentum in China in 2003 when the U.S. auction website, eBay, took a 180 billion USD stake in EachNet—China's online auction leader—and became a major player in the Chinese consumer e-commerce market.[1]

Around the same time, Alibaba, whose site originally made Chinese-made products available to foreign importers, also realized the magnitude of the opportunity that awaited them once online sales became China's new commercial model.[2]

Alibaba.com began as a sort of online Yellow Pages, connecting Chinese manufacturers and trading companies with foreign buyers. If you needed something from China "from a needle to an elephant," as Harrods of London once promised, Alibaba was the place to go.

The model worked so well that people both inside and outside the company were soon wondering whether a domestic version of Alibaba would work too—and under what conditions. Chinese consumers didn't have the established shopping culture known in the West, and its Internet market was still immature.

Alibaba looked with admiration at newcomer eBay. Its model was perfect for an e-commerce startup: a marketplace connecting buyers and sellers. No stock, no warehousing, low fixed costs. Much like Jacky, if Alibaba wanted to launch a successful e-commerce platform in China, it had to differentiate itself from hundreds of local clones. It had to look exotic.

Alibaba knew that Chinese consumers would love eBay's style. But if e-commerce was to be more than a passing fad in China, Alibaba had to tweak eBay's model, adapting its "foreign menu" to domestic tastes.

Porter Erisman, a former Vice President of Alibaba and a key member of founder Jack Ma's Taobao e-commerce team, helped me to understand how the company managed this transition. An American who graduated from Stanford, Porter joined Alibaba in 2000, months before the dotcom bubble collapse that threw Alibaba into crisis. He left the company in 2008, about a year after its triumphant initial public offering on the Hong Kong Stock Exchange. In 2012, he directed "Crocodile in the Yangtze," a documentary about Alibaba's first decade.

As Porter explained, eBay's model, based on auctioning collectibles, didn't adapt well to China. "You had Communism for 30 years. There was nothing to sell, and nobody wanted to buy things second hand. An auction model works with many items to sell and a lot of buyers to compete for them. If you have just a few items to sell, and no buyers, there is no point to an auction."

The Alibaba team understood that the key to developing China-friendly e-commerce lay in helping factories, shops and individuals sell their products online. Consumers wanted to use the Internet to access all kinds of goods, not just collectibles.

The solution would come from Taobao, a C2C (consumer to consumer) website launched in 2003 by Jack Ma, Porter and their team. Unlike Amazon, with its warehouse and fulfillment network, Taobao was simply an enabler, connecting two sides of a transaction. Like eBay, it was a website where people sell to other people.

To build team spirit, Jack Ma asked his Taobao employees to wear military uniforms and fake guns, and organized a massive "war game" in one of Hangzhou's public parks to declare "war" on eBay.

Taobao improved upon the eBay model in several ways. It offered free listings to sellers. It was tailored to the Chinese user, with elements like mascots, puppets and doodles that might seem silly to Western consumers but appeal to the Chinese sensibility.

Another example of team building within Taobao was an internal singing contest similar to *American Idol* in which employees sang songs with phrases like: "The smile of Taobao creates miracles every day . . . new bonds reduce the distance between us! Taobao.com connects us and creates a happy life."[3]

Connection was indeed Taobao's secret weapon; its prawn on the *Risotto alla Milanese.* Taobao's team developed a chat function and other tools to encourage connection between buyers and sellers—creating trust. Though not seen as critical for Western e-commerce, these connections proved key in China, where developing a personal relationship is essential to doing business. Taobao became a combination of Facebook and eBay. "For users in China, eBay seemed too static and minimal," Porter recalled. Within two years, Taobao was China's undisputed market leader. Between 2003 and 2005 its market share surged from 8 percent to 59 percent, while eBay China plunged from 79 percent to 36 percent. By 2006, eBay had shuttered its Chinese site.[4] Game, set, match: Taobao.

The battle between Taobao and eBay for supremacy in the Chinese e-commerce market is legendary, narrated beautifully in Porter's documentary *Crocodile in the Yangtze*. The most important takeaway from eBay's experience, according to Porter, is that: "Imposing a Western model in China doesn't work." He blames eBay's major missed opportunity on the failure to recognize that China's e-commerce model had to be different. "The American auction leader wanted to bring an ideal model to China. However, they should have started from the customer and worked backwards, instead of imposing their model on the Chinese market," he noted.

In other words, they should have come out of the kitchen and taken customers' orders.

As in Jacky's case, Alibaba initially attracted fewer customers than eBay, a famous foreign restaurant with a foreign chef. In fact, e-commerce was initially a foreign concept to the Chinese and in the early days eBay dominated the market. Since consumers did not immediately embrace e-commerce, eBay's Chinese site quickly became a money-loser for an increasingly impatient eBay.

Meanwhile, Taobao, just like Jacky, continued to refine its model to satisfy Chinese tastes, constantly improving and "replacing dishes," and often losing money in the short term, but confident of eventual success. Eventually, consumers migrated from eBay to Taobao, never to return.

The failure of eBay to adapt signaled why China was to become a graveyard for foreign tech companies for years to come.

Chinese e-commerce began using the very same methods its manufacturing companies adopted in the 1990s and 2000s, rapidly adapting existing Western models through continuous iterative cycles until they arrived at something more suited to Chinese customers. This process is called accelerated innovation.[5]

Accelerated innovation is not the revolutionary innovation so highly prized by Silicon Valley. Yet it is equally as important. In fact, China's success has depended on its ability to evolve and scale foreign ideas into mass-market products. This new form of evolution, which is touching the lives of millions, is creating a new kind of revolution in China.

But how exactly does China e-commerce differ from its U.S. counterpart? What makes it so unique?

Digging for Treasure

A few blocks from Jacky's restaurant, Violette, the marketing executive for the U.S.-based entertainment company, is still at work. She has an hour to wait before her conference call with headquarters in New York. Wang Wang, her assistant, has gone out to get food for them both and to take in some fresh air.

Violette and Wang Wang have been working with digital marketing consultants to set up the company's China e-commerce site. Violette will need to explain to headquarters—once again—that Chinese customers buy in a unique way and therefore the site needs to be tailored to the Chinese market. She has been experiencing resistance because her company is in a hurry to launch e-commerce sites not only in China, but in Malaysia, Singapore and Indonesia as well. To save time and money, they want to standardize their site and its operations.

Things are quiet in the office. Violette has some time to kill while she waits for the conference call. She grabs her iPad and logs onto a popular video game. A pop-up window opens: the home page of JD.com, one of China's biggest online direct-sales companies. Suddenly, she recalls the pink-and-black sneakers she saw at the gym. She pauses the game and scrolls down JD.com's page. On the left side she finds the sneaker section. Then a flash sale banner for handbags distracts her.

She opens the page, but none of the bags appeals to her. She returns to the sneaker section to see whether there is a promotion. Finding none, she visits another company, VIP.com, a top Chinese flash sales site. No sales for those sneakers on that site either, but she does see a sale for pearl earrings, handmade in Suzhou, a region famous for its pearls. The discount makes the item irresistible. After a quick online chat with the vendor, she clicks on the item and checks out. By tomorrow evening, she'll have them in hand.

The first major difference between Chinese e-commerce and its U.S. counterpart is that, unlike in the West, where the Internet is used mainly to search for things, in China, the Internet is a primary form of entertainment. Some call it the "entertainment superhighway." So Chinese e-commerce needs to amuse and entertain customers, just like a video game.

When people go online and start looking around, they literally say they are "playing the Internet." In Mandarin, looking around is pronounced *wan-er*, meaning to "play" or "entertain." During her free time, Violette isn't really shopping for sneakers. She is not really shopping for anything in particular. She is entertaining herself by looking around.

It is not by chance that China's most successful e-commerce site is called Taobao, Chinese for "digging for treasure." Shopping is a game, by definition.

Digging for treasure is not rational procurement; it is a form of play. "Playing" might include browsing, and may result in a purchase, but often the purchase is not the result of a plan to buy. Purchase occurs while one is killing time on a bus, on the subway, or waiting for a conference call. It is an intrinsically spontaneous activity.

When I first encountered Chinese e-commerce, I could not really grasp the difference between a consumer's shopping research and gaming. Being an avid Google user, looking up things online is a kind of entertainment for me. Watching a video on YouTube, looking for hotels, flights, restaurants—these are all forms of entertainment. I could not understand how the Chinese Internet and its e-commerce could be so different from the West. That is, until I met someone who introduced me to the world of Chinese online gaming and virtual reality.

* * *

One of the most distinctive facets of the French Concession's architectural heritage is its lane houses, or *longtong*, a fusion of Chinese courtyards and Western row houses. They are normally three stories tall and four meters wide. They are organized in a dense, grid-like pattern with east–west and north–south lanes.

On the third floor of a beautiful *longtong*, I met Toine Rooijmans, veteran of China's Internet, and co-lecturer of IT Management at the Hult Business School in Shanghai. I went to his office to learn more about e-commerce and its close relationship with online gaming. Toine and his business partner, Onno, greeted me at the door.

We walked past an open space into a meeting room. The light wooden floors and white furniture created a serene environment in contrast to the urban hum just outside of the office.

Young Chinese employees were working at their computers. "It's Dining City, our website," said Toine. Dining City helps users book tables and provides information on fine dining in several cities around China. "We're the OpenTable of Shanghai,"[6] Onno explained helpfully.

Suddenly, Toine's dog came towards us. He wanted to play. Toine gave him a little toy to keep him busy. We moved to the meeting room and sat down. I opened my Moleskine ready to take notes. The dog was looking at us through the glass door. He was curious, maybe because he knew I was about to hear one of the most fascinating stories I had been told so far.

Originally from Holland, Toine is slim, shorthaired and a quick thinker. He is wearing a pair of jeans, a polo shirt, blue blazer and brown leather shoes. He likes to be comfortable at work, but also smartly dressed.

Toine has been living in China since 2006 and has seen many changes during that time. His first internship was with a Chinese gaming company that developed online games, similar to the one played by Violette. He was responsible for conducting market research and profiling game users for the company.

After that internship, Toine joined a Korean company developing a 3D platform to support gaming, e-commerce and education. Toine's job was to figure out a way to bring traffic to their virtual-world website, and ensure that customers would buy and receive their purchased items on time. What he learned during those years is at the core of today's Chinese e-commerce business models.

One of Toine's market research tasks was to interview the game users and learn their behaviors. He discovered that the Chinese have a very different type of psychology than Westerners when it comes to the Internet. In the West, people use the Internet to search for information and learn about things. In China, however, people use it primarily to entertain themselves. In China, people will play any-thing, anywhere, at any time of day; even when doing other tasks. Boredom was, and still is, what drives most people to the Internet in China.

To understand the full extent to which "play" triumphs over "search," in China, Toine would ask his subjects simply: "How did you learn about our website?" He learned that the users were finding the site through word of mouth or blogs. He would then ask if users were searching online for things they did not know. The answer was always the same: "When we do not know something, we ask our friends."

"What if your friends do not know?" Toine would follow up. "Then, nobody knows," they would answer.

Another fundamental aspect separates Chinese Internet culture from that of the West. In China the offline real world can be so unattractive that the online virtual world becomes the best escape from a gloomy reality. This is especially true for hundreds of millions of factory workers.

China's entertainment industry does little to compete with the online world. TV programs are so highly controlled that they don't really appeal to a younger audience. In fact, it's common to find young people who have never watched TV.[7] The Internet is their primary means of communication and entertainment. As a result, the online world has become the real center of cultural innovation in modern China.

Toine and Onno's story reminded me of Violette's shopping experience—the very habits she is about to explain to headquarters in New York. A big danger for Western brands is thinking that entering the Chinese online market is as simple as launching a retooled version of their main site: translating the contents of their pages into Chinese, adding "Asian" faces, or changing the site's color palette. But that is only a small part of the equation. The other, more important factor to consider is that Chinese go online for entertainment—to shop, play games and to "dig for treasure."

Chinese, in fact, buy in a very unique way.

One Thousand and One Clicks

One Thousand and One Nights is the well-known collection of West and South Asian stories and folk tales, compiled in Arabic, known in English as the Arabian Nights. Numerous stories depict sorcerers, magicians, legendary places and exotic bazaars carrying thousands of products.

When looking at Chinese main e-commerce platforms like Tao-bao, Tmall, JD.com, or Yihaodian the resemblance to a digital version of an exotic bazaar is striking.

According to a report by the McKinsey Global Institute (MGI), in China 90 percent of online retail is sold through these kinds of uniquely Chinese marketplaces.[8] In the U.S., the marketplace share is only one-third of that of China—around 24 percent. Loaded with goods and suppliers, the Alibaba marketplace is for the moment, at least, the winning model in China. It gives a bazaar feel, and is intrinsically playful and interesting.

Chinese have been doing business in bazaars across the world for centuries. Bazaars first appeared along the important trade routes, and were among the reasons cities arose and prospered.[9] The word "bazaar" comes from the Persian *vazar*, meaning a commercial zone where one can buy or exchange goods and services.[10]

Chinese bazaars rapidly became areas not only for the trading of goods, but were also the social, religious, and financial centers of cities—think of Socrates and the Athenian agora. Hence, bazaars have stronger historical and cultural identities than Western malls.

Today, midway through the second decade of the new millennium, the Chinese can build a 15-story building in 48 hours. There are over 1.2 billion mobile phones users, and some of the world's fastest high-speed trains race across the country's vast distances. However, certain habits and expectations remain distinctly Chinese and have not changed, despite modernity.

The Chinese bazaar is one of those, and the digital marketplace is really just its 3.0 version. It shares many features with the Chinatowns found across the world, from Russia to San Francisco to Panama City. Through the centuries, the Chinese have not only perfected the bazaar model and carried it beyond their national borders, but they have now upgraded it to a successful cyber version: the "one thousand and one clicks" bazaar.

Time and again Chinese bazaars have proven formidable competitors to indigenous businesses and merchants.[11] The digital bazaar—the online souk—has many of the same advantages of the ancient bazaar: it creates competition among vendors, thus driving down prices. It also allows people to engage merchants in conversation, providing them with feedback on pricing and quality.

Another consequence is that shops operating outside the bazaar are likely to appear to buyers as riskier sources of product. This is why, rather than shopping from individual sites, such as Tory Burch or Prada.com, Chinese prefer bazaars.

Violette, like many Chinese consumers, might refer to a company's main site to look at the newest products, but not to make a purchase. Bazaars are perceived as highly social entities whereas individual brand websites in China seem "antisocial" and therefore untrustworthy—at least for the moment.

What modern factors help make the digital bazaar so successful? According to a *Financial Times* article, shopping in China can be a pretty stressful experience. Normally shoppers have two options. They can travel to department stores where they find expensive Western products, often made in China, or they can go to markets where they risk being overcharged for goods that are not always authentic.

"Through an old-fashioned yet ultra-modern shopping experience, digital platforms have taken the nightmare of shopping and transformed it into a painless, virtual experience. Visually, the Alibaba site might seem as cluttered as a downtown bazaar—but with far more convenience and little of the hassle."[12]

In China, marketplace operators provide a central website, a place in cyberspace where small and medium enterprises and microbusinesses can sell any sort of product. Low overhead costs and rival e-merchants keep prices competitive.

During a lecture at the Stanford Business School, Jack Ma explained: "You might see a t-shirt in a shop that costs 150 USD, and find it on Taobao for 15 USD. How can that be possible, assuming that you want to buy an original product? Because selling offline requires a lot of fees—advertising, distribution—that drive costs up . . . We teach consumers to be smart, and we are connecting businesses with consumers."[13]

Platforms have made consumption convenient and entertaining for the bored Chinese shopper. They have given customers better information about products and pricing and made it more difficult for monopolistic sellers to overcharge consumers.

In other words, they have created a system that ensures trust.

When Violette was browsing for earrings online and found a pair she liked, she immediately opened a dialogue window to chat with the merchant. They chatted a while before sealing the purchase. They were building trust. Once Violette felt comfortable, she placed the order.

If the merchant does his job properly, after two or three hitch-free transactions, Violette will purchase without the same level of engagement. The reason? The merchant has gained her trust. Once trust is established, purchases are more likely and more frequent. The future orders are also likely to be larger.

Now imagine thousands, hundreds of thousands of transactions all going through the same bazaar. Buyer comments—thousands of them—are posted every day. Just about everything you could hope to know about that vendor or their product is available on your screen. Virtue is rewarded in this system, and trust keeps the gears of marketplace e-commerce greased. Asymmetries of information are reduced, and everyone benefits.

An individual stand-alone site simply cannot compete against a marketplace that is deemed trustworthy.

But what are these platforms and how do they work?

CHAPTER 3

A New Breed of Companies

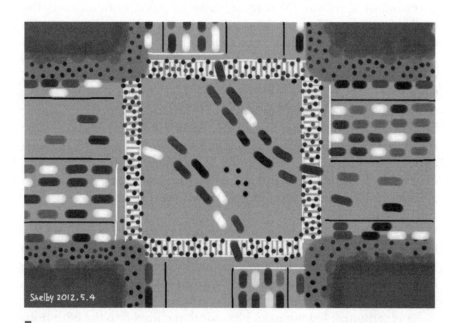

Shelby 2012.5.4

In 1995, Jack Ma is in the waiting room of one of Beijing's many ministries discussing with two bureaucrats from the Communist Party. One is wearing a gray suit and the other an acetate suit. The first one walks over to him. Jack Ma, in typical Chinese etiquette, stands up, slightly bows, and proffers his business card with both hands. He is there to "promote China on the 'information superhighway'." Back then the word Internet had not been used yet, so he alludes to a highway to make the bureaucrats understand what he means. Both officers look puzzled.

The man wearing the acetate suit is smoking and staring at the ground. He could not be less interested. The scene shifts to Jack Ma seated in front of a computer, showing the two Party men the site he has created and wants to launch. It is called China Pages. Ma explains that there are very limited contents on the Internet on China. "We can do better than the Americans," he says.

The two bureaucrats look at him, nodding and truly without any idea of what he means.

Later, Jack Ma talks about his superhighway to another official. He hopes that this person might understand what Ma is trying to do. He says that his site is ready, but the Web pages are still blank; he needs government approval. "You must make an appointment," says the bureaucrat. "It is protocol. If you do not make an appointment, it is difficult to give an adequate response."

Jack Ma's China Pages will close a few months later. After a few months working as a technician in a stifling office at the Ministry of Commerce, he will set up his next business: Alibaba.com.[1]

At the closing bell on September 19, 2014, the date of its historic initial public offering on the NYSE, Alibaba Group's market value stood at 231 billion USD,[2] larger than fellow tech giants Facebook and Amazon and U.S. household names such as JP Morgan and Procter & Gamble.[3] Were it an American company, it would be among the ten biggest for its market value, *The Wall Street Journal* calculated.

On a Monday afternoon in November, I crossed Hong Kong Bay to Kowloon where I headed to the ICC building to meet with Vikram Malhotra who heads Credit Suisse Group Investment Banking for Asia Pacific. Credit Suisse played a leading role in Alibaba's 20 billion plus USD initial public offering (IPO).

A receptionist led me to an elevator that climbed to the 88th floor lobby. Through a maze of corridors, meeting rooms, statues and paintings, I finally arrived in the Karachi room facing Hong Kong's misty bay. Dressed in a blue suit, checkered shirt and Shanghai Tang cufflinks, Vik extended his hand and warmly introduced himself. "Hi, my name is Vik." Vik is a popular figure at Credit Suisse, having worked for the bank for 25 years. We sat down, I opened my notepad and he agreed to take me behind the scenes of one of the world's biggest IPOs.

"It was one of the best executed IPOs we have ever done, from kick-off to listing," said Vik. I learned that the IPO is the result of a four-year effort. "It was a project that definitely did not happen overnight," said Vik.

Since 2011, Vik and his team have been working hard to help Alibaba climb to the top of the e-commerce market. He told me about some of the most important steps to get to the September IPO. In 2012, his team worked on five mergers and acquisitions and financing transactions for Alibaba. Credit Suisse was the lead adviser for Alibaba's share buyback from Yahoo and advised on the move to take Alibaba.com private after its listing in Hong Kong in 2007.[4]

"The 8.3 billion USD share buyback was the biggest loan transaction for a tech company. It required judgment and thought," explained Vik. "To achieve that financing was not an easy task. In 2012, when Facebook got listed, the markets were very tough. We had to twist several arms to make it happen and invested in Alibaba ourselves. We put our money where our mouth was and this built the foundation for the IPO."

According to Vik, Alibaba's performance was even more fundamental for the IPO's success. "I think that what people are doing at Alibaba is mesmerizing. They know their mission and live by it. They want to challenge the status quo and make a difference."

"Thanks to Alibaba, China is leapfrogging from no shopping to online shopping and Silicon Valley is now acknowledging China's Internet companies' important role," said Vik. "With this IPO, the fresh air of the Hangzhou Lake is giving oxygen to Silicon Valley," he said, referring to Yahoo and its strategic investment in Alibaba.

The Internet Cowboys

Alibaba's story is a bit like China's Internet story; it begins with a search with no results. "Jack was not the first Internet entrepreneur to succeed in China," Porter said during an interview with Italian journalist Eugenio Cau.[5] "His success came after many attempts." But Jack Ma is a pioneer who traveled the country and convinced Chinese entrepreneurs to go online. "He brought China into the age of the Internet," said Porter.

From its early, experimental days in 1995, China set a clear direction for its Internet. It was not aimed at creating a society based on the creation and use of information as it was in the U.S. Instead, it had to serve a knowledge economy based on intellectual capabilities, a shift away from physical labor or natural resources.[6]

China needed the Internet to upgrade from a pure manufacturing economy to a service economy. It did not need it to spread information around.

However, China didn't have the capacity to build its own Internet. So it sought external help. Groups of Chinese who had studied in the U.S. (the famous "sea turtles," or *haigui*) were crossing the Pacific and returning to China to set up their dotcoms.[7] It was the first gold rush, the first listings, and the go-go days with venture capital money flowing into the Chinese Internet.[8] These were the days when Yahoo and its founder, Jerry Yang, were seen as the benchmarks.

The vast majority of Chinese Internet companies chose U.S. capital markets as their preferred destination for listing. This was due to the relative newness of the Internet and the immaturity of Asian capital markets when it came to the tech sector. Billy Wong, partner of the Corporate Group of Orrick, Herrington & Sutcliffe LLP in Hong Kong, a well-known international law firm advising technology companies in Silicon Valley, told me, "Many Chinese and Asian Internet companies (gaming, e-commerce, etc.) chose to be listed in the U.S. because Asian markets were initially less mature when it came to understanding how to list tech companies. In recent years, however, some Chinese tech companies have chosen to list on the local PRC stock market, often attracted by the fact that valuations tended to be much higher. Questions have arisen, however, whether many A-share listed company's valuations really reflect their fundamentals. Given the market crash in China during summer 2015, we have seen issuers starting to rethink whether the PRC stock market is the right listing platform in the longer term."

"The mid- to late-2000s were really the Internet cowboy days," exclaimed Toine, Dining City's co-founder. "It all happened very fast! I recall examining the half-year subscription data reports and seeing that every minute in China, the equivalent of a European village was coming online for the first time. These were people who had never been on the Internet before, who did not even know what it was." Toine speculated that "This vast, growing army of newbies was most likely in an Internet café, surfing hao123.com, a listing portal owned by Baidu and one of the most popular sites in the world,[9] and playing online games."

According to Toine, the Internet in China was initially the province of the young, but it quickly spread to other parts of the population. "Next, you had high-end, middle- and low-end users. And then, as cities developed, it became even more segmented: tier one, tier two, third and fourth tier users," recalled Toine. "Every time we did research, I knew we would have to do it again in six months. The market was changing very fast."

In those years, a plethora of Chinese Internet companies were launched, matured and died in super-short cycles. "When looking at these cycles, you could see how fast these companies changed their products to fit their users. It was like nothing I'd ever seen before," Toine marveled. This was China's accelerated innovation at its core.

"Literally, users were doing one thing one day and another thing the following day," said Toine. "Some guy would see inefficiencies and decide to do something about it. If successful, he would be rich very fast. Soon, he would be gone and another guy would take his place to solve another problem and so forth." It's mind-boggling to see what people did in China with almost no resources.

Toine told me the story of David Li and his company YY.com, a major Chinese video-based social network with hundreds of millions of users. David, an avid online game player, launched his company in 2005 as a gaming portal. At the time, David was frustrated with the quality of Voice Over Internet Protocol for game chat in China. For example, when playing World of Warcraft, poor voice quality would make it annoying to coordinate an attack with fellow gamers.

In 2008, David developed a communication service, enabling gamers to voice and text chat over the Internet in real time. Suddenly, all gamers moved onto his platform. Next, he created virtual singing rooms, where aspiring artists could give virtual private concerts and people could donate virtual currency to artists who could then convert it into cash. Soon, singers from the remote Chinese country-side were cashing in using this platform. "A young guy created a function and made a fortune by solving inefficiency," said Toine. YY got listed on the NASDAQ in 2012 and was invested in, among others, by Lei Jun, Xiaomi's co-founder.

"Looking at these stories, you realize how quickly the Chinese Internet developed," said Toine. The key to this development is the Chinese willingness to adopt new trends and new things, and to let go of existing structures. "In a blink of an eye," Toine explained, "I saw China going from a country where 'nobody is really online' to millions of people playing video games. Then people started buying virtual goods online, but there were no payments systems. Then, everybody had a smartphone and the billion-dollar e-commerce market happened. Now we have platforms like Alibaba, JD.com and Yihaodian with fully integrated offerings and same-day delivery," said Toine.

"It is pretty much unimaginable that this has happened in just ten years. It has been a crazy ride," said Toine. And even if the wild "cowboy days" have ended, and things have become more standardized, he insisted, "It is still a very exciting time. A lot of innovation is still happening here out of necessity. From a certain perspective, China is still a developing country and there are a lot of opportunities to improve and build new things."

A tour of some of the key companies that have shaped China's Internet economy is in order to help understand what Toine finds so "unimaginable."

BAT and the X Factor

Chinese Internet companies have consolidated into three main Internet players known as "BAT": Baidu, Alibaba and Tencent. They are massive platforms, and they are all Chinese. Each platform comes from a different city in China, Beijing, Hangzhou and Shenzhen, respectively.

However, industry experts believe there are a small number of other companies who could soon reach huge market capitalization and become new challengers to the "BAT status." JP Gan, one of the top venture capitalists in China, believes that "It now makes sense to talk about an X factor, in other words, a BAT-*X*. The X represents the next big platform."

The first time I heard about JP's BAT-X theory was during a banking conference. I wanted to learn more about it, so I reached out to JP to ask for a meeting. We met at his office in Shanghai where he heads Qiming Venture Partners, an early growth stage venture capital firm. Since its debut in 2006, Qiming Ventures has become one of the leading investment firms in China managing four funds with over 1.7 billion USD in assets.[10] I asked JP what it takes to become the X.

"You have to be the best at what you do; competition is fierce in China," JP explained. Looking, for example, at BAT, Baidu excels at search, Alibaba at e-commerce, and Tencent at gaming and social.

Each one has a specialty, a predefined DNA. JP gave me two examples of companies that could one day become the X in the X factor: JD.com and Xiaomi. "They both want to be the X, and in terms of market capitalization they are really big, but this is not enough to become the X. You have to create your own market and build an ecosystem of interconnected services," said JP. "I believe that if JD. com excels at B2C e-commerce, it can build its ecosystem thus becoming the X. Xiaomi is also working very hard to create its own market and ecosystem. It is one of the most worthy companies on the planet." The race has just begun.

While JP was explaining his theory, I could not help thinking that, while some of the most famous Chinese Internet companies have been founded and built by many U.S.-trained Chinese managers, ironically American Internet companies have not yet been successful in China. There are several explanations for this.

"Chinese entrepreneurs behave differently, respond to other instincts, and assess different market needs which Westerners often do not understand," said Porter when talking to Italian journalist Eugenio Cau. "Chinese technology companies tend to move even faster than their Silicon Valley counterparts; they are more willing to make mistakes and then move in new directions."

There are also deeper reasons for the failure of Western tech companies in China. As I was told by Krzysztof Werkun, an investment banker with deep mergers and acquisitions experience in both Silicon Valley and China: "Entrepreneurship is in the Chinese DNA."

Krzysztof works with Hong Kong's China Renaissance Partners, one of the largest independent boutique investment banks, helping Chinese tech companies sell shares in the U.S. and an underwriter of JD.com's 1.5 billion USD IPO. He regularly works with Chinese entrepreneurs and believes that managers sent by foreign companies to launch startups in China are competing against the world's best entrepreneurs, who are known for "squeezing water out of rocks." "American companies use advanced, sophisticated 'developed country' models and find them too hard to scale to a developing market, which is immature by definition," he told me.

"It is hard for Western tech companies to put together a startup team in China," Krzysztof explained. "Often local managers see opportunities but are unable to pursue them because of the way the headquarters runs the business. Global companies tend to push one-size-fits-all solutions while to succeed in China you need to localize your strategy. Eventually local managers become frustrated and strike out on their own or join local startups."

According to Porter, the corporate culture at Western tech companies is often out of tune with the Chinese workforce. "Chinese startups tend to focus much more on the group. Western startups are more individualistic," Porter told a reporter. "When I was at Alibaba, sometimes it felt like being part of a family."

Alibaba is the benchmark of Chinese tech companies' culture. To reinforce the spirit of camaraderie at annual corporate events, Jack Ma is famous for wearing funny costumes from fairy tales characters to rock stars. In fact, Alibaba takes its name from a famous fairy tale.

Alibaba (Hangzhou)

Ali Baba is a character from the folk tale *Ali Baba and the Forty Thieves*, one of the best-known stories from *One Thousand and One Nights*. In the story, Ali Baba is a poor woodcutter who discovers a fortune when he opens the door to a chamber of treasures using the magic words, "Open Sesame."

When Jack Ma was trying to decide on a name for his new company, he wanted to make sure the name he chose would be globally recognized. One morning at a coffee shop in San Francisco, he asked his waitress if she knew the story of Ali Baba.

She replied immediately: "Yes . . . Open Sesame."[11] He took to the street and asked 30 people from all over the world the same question. They all knew the story: Ali Baba. Open Sesame. Jack Ma knew he had found his name. Indeed, the Alibaba Group opened the door to fortunes for a new wave of small- to medium-sized Chinese companies.

Alibaba is now the largest e-commerce group in the world. In 2014, its platforms handled transactions totaling 270 billion USD. Its revenues for the year 2014 were equal to 12.29 billion USD (Amazon totaled over 88 billion USD). Alibaba has over 367 million active users.[12]

Taobao and Tmall generate the majority of the revenues for the Alibaba Group. Taobao is the ninth most-visited website globally,[13] and earns revenue from advertising by its more than 7 million sellers. Tmall (Chinese name *Tian Mao*), introduced in 2008, is a B2C (business to consumer) platform for large companies such Nike, Gap and Levi's. Brands offer products directly to the public and pay a deposit and commission on each transaction. Together, Tmall and Taobao represent 80 percent of China's e-commerce market.

At the beginning of 2014, Apple decided to open its own Tmall "virtual store," a striking confirmation of the importance of this platform. In February 2014, Tmall Global was born, a new online marketplace based in Hong Kong, which allows international companies to sell to Chinese consumers without needing a legal entity in China.

To better understand the appeal of Alibaba's platforms, I spoke with Violette and Fan Fan, an entrepreneur who set up a small online fashion empire selling both on Taobao and Tmall. Fan Fan explained, "From a seller's point of view you can start from Taobao, but eventually you move to Tmall because there is simply too much competition on Taobao. Tmall is more careful with brands, and it cares about having authentic vendors and products."

Fan Fan noticed that in the last few years many people have left their jobs to start Taobao shops. Due to the low entry barriers for sellers, Taobao is an easy target for fake products. "If a customer sees the same clothes on Tmall or Taobao she would rather buy on Tmall," said Fan Fan. Between 2009 and 2011 Taobao established significant controls to largely address this problem.

For Violette, Taobao's variety of products is simply unmatched. This can be great—or not. "You can find everything on Taobao, but too much choice means that purchasing can take hours. Besides, you have to check the vendor's references and feedback to avoid buying fakes." Violette finds shopping on Tmall easier: "You know that there is often a real brand and shop behind it, for example, Burberry or Apple Tmall original stores. Trust saves a lot of time."

Lack of trust was indeed blocking e-commerce growth. To address this barrier, Alibaba introduced Alipay in 2004, a kind of Chinese PayPal with a unique and critical feature. In Alipay's online payment system, a third party vets the claims made by sellers. For example, John wants to buy from Steven, but doesn't want to pay without seeing the goods. Steven doesn't want to ship the product before being paid. John sends money from his bank account directly to Alipay. If he is happy with the product, Alipay releases the funds to Steven. If John is not happy with the product and returns it, Alipay refunds his money.

Another unique Alipay feature is that it takes money upfront and puts it in an escrow account. Vendors are thus assured that payments made through Alipay will be honored.

Alipay really took off in 2008, when Jack Ma, like Steve Jobs with iTunes and the major players of the music industry, found a way to sit all the big banks around a table and agree on one simple payment system. As Porter noted, "It takes a visionary entrepreneur to make that happen."

Alipay was single-handedly responsible for transitioning the growth of Chinese e-commerce from linear to exponential. Going back to the concept of how technology develops, in the early stages, linear and exponential growth look alike. Exponential growth is not instantaneous. However, once the X factor kicks in, growth becomes explosive. This is exactly what happened with Alipay. From 2003 to 2008, China e-commerce grew almost linearly. That graph shot up like a hockey stick after the arrival of Alipay.

Alipay turned out to be more than a very efficient online payment system: it is now used by Alibaba to connect the online world to the offline. Every connection Alibaba creates between these two worlds goes through Alipay.

Tencent (Shenzhen)

Ask people to list the world's biggest technology companies and they will tell you: Google, Amazon and Facebook. One name almost certainly won't come up, though it has every right to stand shoulder to shoulder with the best the Web has to offer. The company? Tencent.

Tencent offers social networking, messaging (Tencent QQ), Web portals (QQ.com, one of China's largest), e-commerce, payment systems (TenPay) and multiplayer online games.[14]

Now the world's fourth-largest Internet company[15] (after Google, Amazon and eBay) and eighth in traffic worldwide,[16] Tencent is listed on the Hong Kong Stock Exchange with capitalization in the hundreds of billions of dollars. Its president, Ma Huateng (Pony Ma in English), is the Mark Zuckerberg of China. He began in the mid-2000s with online gaming, and then the company grew to other platforms. China is now the world's biggest online gaming market.

In May 2014, at the Beijing Global Mobile Internet Conference, Tencent COO Marc Ren announced his company's ambitious goal: "To connect the offline with the online world." Tencent is poised to become one of the biggest players in the world of the Internet of Things.

Like Alibaba, Tencent uses a tool to bridge the physical and virtual worlds: WeChat and its payment system TenPay.

Launched in 2011, WeChat, or *Weixin* in Mandarin, meaning "little message," is a fully integrated mobile-only social application and media platform, the very same one that Violette uses to call her cab and pay for her ride. It is Tencent's secret weapon.

WeChat is a combination of Facebook and WhatsApp, and has hundreds of millions of users. Beyond messaging, its offerings include a mobile news reading application, a blogging platform, an online storefront and a mobile wallet.

As of September 2015, WeChat had over 570 million daily logged-in users. The daily amount of WeChat video and voice calls equals 280 million minutes, which is about 540 years! The average WeChat user reads the equivalent of one full novel per month on WeChat. It is simply humongous.[17]

According to a Credit Lyonnais Securities Asia (CLSA) research study,[18] WeChat's innovative suite of services has already surpassed those of the U.S.'s WhatsApp. WeChat and the Japanese messaging application, Line, are likely to dominate in Asia, and could challenge their U.S. peers in other markets.[19]

WeChat growth isn't limited to China; it is quickly spreading beyond its borders. It already has over 100 million users in other countries. To enter the Hispanic language market in 2013, WeChat spent 200 million USD on advertising, enlisting a celebrity endorsement from Barcelona football ace Lionel Messi.

Baidu (Beijing)

Baidu is the leading search engine in Mandarin. *Baidu*, whose literal meaning is "hundreds of times," represents the persistent search for the ideal. Its name was inspired by a poem written over 800 years ago, during the Song Dynasty. The company controls 80 percent of the Internet's Chinese-language search market. Though apparently resembling Google—it is often called the "Google of China"—the comparison can be misleading.

To understand what makes Baidu tick I traveled to Beijing to meet with Kaiser Kuo—Baidu's director for International Communications. Kaiser is definitely a well-known character in Beijing. His parents are both Chinese, who left the mainland during the civil war emigrating first to Taiwan and then to the U.S. He grew up in different parts of the U.S. where he received a Western education. His parents remained pro-mainland China, even after relocating to the U.S., and traveled to their home country with Kaiser and his siblings in the early 1980s. This was the time when he decided to invest more time to learn the language and the culture properly. He has been living in Beijing since 1996 working as a technology correspondent, a journalist and in digital marketing, and finally joined Baidu in 2010. He is the author of a well-known podcast called Sinica where he invites prominent China journalists and China-watchers to participate in uncensored discussions about Chinese political and economic affairs. In other words, if you want to know what happens in the Chinese tech sphere, look for him.

My meeting with Kaiser started in quite an entertaining way. When I reached the Baidu campus, I asked the front desk lady to inform him that I had arrived. She told me that there was no Kaiser at Baidu. I believed that knowing his Chinese name would have helped her to locate him, but everyone calls him Kaiser. So I decided to explain to her who he was. Before becoming a journalist Kaiser was part of a well-known band. I told her that he used to be a part-time musician. The lady turned to her colleague whispering in her ear whether I was looking for the rock-guy-with-long-hair. I told her: "that's him!" She smiled and said that his name is Guo YiGuang. There it was, Kaiser's Chinese name.

I sat down in the big hall and waited for Kaiser, or Mr Guo, to pick me up. He recognized me immediately. I guess I was the only person wearing a suit in a place populated by software engineers wearing jeans and t-shirts—apparently my lawyer habits are still embedded in my dress code. We walked to the escalator and up to the fifth floor. We sat in one of the open spaces and he brought me up to speed with what Baidu was, is and will be. As usual, a 30-minute conversation turned into a much longer discussion of what is happening in the e-commerce world.

"A lot of people compare Baidu to Google, does it still apply?" I asked Kaiser to start our interview. "I understand why people do that. Sometimes you need to explain something unknown in an easy way and a comparison can help," said Kaiser. "In the past there were many similarities. Both were the predominant search engines in their respective markets. Both are engineering-led companies. For example, if you are a talented engineer in the U.S. you want to work for Google and the same happens in China, but other than that the product lines are very different now; what the companies do, our missions, our cultures, etc. are different. Right now we are at the point where this comparison obscures more than it illuminates," said Kaiser.

Baidu ranks fourth overall in Alexa traffic rankings,[20] and was listed on the NASDAQ in 2005. It offers a Wikipedia-like communal encyclopedia, Baidu Baike, and a discussion forum.[21] Its CEO, Li Yanhong, is the Chinese Larry Page. In the U.S., where he worked as a computer engineer, he's known as Robin Li.

The reason why Kaiser thinks that the comparison is misleading is that starting from 2011 Baidu has shifted from its previous desktop search model. Chinese Internet has migrated towards mobile and Baidu had to follow, and eventually lead. For Baidu the future was not just about search—still a vital and important area for Baidu—but it was also very much about services. Search advertising was definitely big—Baidu controls one-third of China's online advertising market of around 24.2 billion USD[22]—but services and the retail market will be even bigger. According to Kaiser: "Baidu now focuses on connecting people to services through its search engine, and through online-to-offline (O2O) services both domestically and internationally." In a nutshell: "Baidu differs from Google because it focuses on local on-demand services," says Kaiser.

"We started to evolve from our traditional model when we saw that people who used to come to Baidu to look for information were more and more looking for services. Once we had become dominant in mobile search the next step was obvious. We reached the right height to see what could be done next and the answer was O2O," says Kaiser.

Since 2011 the company has been investing 5 billion of its 12 billion USD cash reserves[23] into offline services. In the last two years it has made more than ten investments including the 169 million USD stake in a startup called Nuomi Holdings Inc., which has become the platform for on-site services such as dining, movie tickets and karaoke. Baidu has declared that it will invest 3.1 billion USD in Nuomi over three years.[24] Baidu has also developed a separate platform called Baidu Takeout Delivery (in Chinese: *Baidu Wai Mai*) operating a fleet of contracted electric-bike riders delivering anything edible. Finally, Baidu has invested in Qunar, an online airline and reservation portal listed in 2013 on the NASDAQ.

"When we first sized the market we saw that it was an enormous opportunity. In these three areas that we have just talked about—

Nuomi, Takeout Delivery and Qunar—we sized that market alone to 10 trillion RMB," says Kaiser.

Baidu's shift from a Google-like model to services has also happened for another reason: Chinese Internet has different characteristics compared to that of the U.S. According to Andrew Ng, chief scientist at Baidu U.S., and the head of the company's research wing in Silicon Valley: "When searching for a movie ticket on Google or Bing, both sites can send you to a website called Fandango—a movie ticket site. However, in China the system is different because [in the past] Baidu could not send the user anywhere, the ticket booking website did not exist yet. Baidu had to buiid it first. If Baidu wants certain types of Internet to exist to improve the user experience, it needs to *make that Internet.* The Chinese Internet ecosystem is less developed, there's a greater burden on search engine," Mr Ng said.[25] This is why the company has become so deeply involved in offline services.

In the mobile world age, Baidu is creating a gigantic ecosystem that can easily plug into his search engine and eventually create something that one day a billion people will use.

In September 2014 Baidu and Tencent formed an alliance to develop an O2O platform in China. This alliance polarized the Chinese Internet market: on one side Alibaba and on the other side Baidu and Tencent. It is basically Hangzhou against the rest of China.[26]

Several non-BAT companies in China's e-commerce market are also important to mention as they are among the biggest contenders for the X factor in BAT-X.

JD.com (Beijing)

Alibaba's main e-commerce competitor is JD.com. Ironically, I learned its 40-year-old founder and CEO's story from an article in *Corriere Della Sera*, the most popular Italian newspaper. He is definitely famous in Italy too.

Liu Qiangdong came from a family of wealthy landowners swept away by the Communist Revolution. His childhood was very humble and "at home we ate rice once or twice a week. Meat was a dream," he remembered. "But I was very good in school and I was passionate about technology." Though of modest origins, he was very resourceful and to support himself at university, he addressed envelopes for hire charging 3 yuan cents per envelope, up to 60,000 per month, for a total of 1–2,000 yuan a month. At that time a typical factory worker would earn a 300 yuan salary. Liu used the savings to purchase a phone and a computer. His first venture was a restaurant, which failed miserably. Then he sold pirated DVDs. Soon he realized that he could use the Internet to sell not only DVDs but also almost any other kind of product.[27]

JD.com is China's biggest online direct sales company and the second largest e-commerce company after Alibaba,[28] with over 600 million users. Its business model is similar to that of Amazon, and its strength lies in its fulfillment infrastructure and mobile. JD.com has built an extensive warehouse network, as well as a delivery team to enhance last-mile services. It has multiple warehouses in China's main cities, and thousands of employees dedicated to delivery. JD.com was listed on the NASDAQ in May 2014.

Thanks to its partnership with Alibaba's archrival Tencent, JD.com is also strong in mobile. JD.com has become the default e-commerce site for WeChat. Tencent needs JD.com to succeed in order to enrich its services on WeChat and compete against Alibaba. Thanks to this partnership, Shenzhen and Beijing are now getting even closer.

Xiaomi (Beijing)

Xiaomi is one of China's biggest tech companies, and now the world's most highly valued technology startup.[29] It employs roughly 7,000 people and has a market value equal to three times Lenovo's, the IBM of China. Not only does it develop software but it also designs, develops and sells smartphones and consumer electronics. Since the release of its first smartphone in August 2011, Xiaomi has gained an incredible market share in China.

Sales are conducted online, saving 25–30 percent on distribution costs, which can, in turn, be used to develop newer phone versions. Once the products are sold, Xiaomi listens carefully to its user feedback applying small changes to the product throughout its lifecycle.

Xiaomi positions itself as an aspirational brand for the lower income consumer. It does not compete for market share with iPhone; rather it is targeted to the masses. Although it is a hardware producer, Xiaomi's eclectic business model makes it a company that behaves like a Silicon Valley Internet company.

I met Hugo Barra, Vice President of Xiaomi Global, in Jakarta during the November Startup Asia event. Dressed in a black t-shirt, dark jeans and flashy orange sneakers, he gave me some insight into Xiaomi's business model. Hugo comes from Brazil and was a Google key player in Android. In 2013, he left Google to move to Xiaomi and become a VP. According to Hugo, "My parents and 50 percent of my friends thought that this was a crazy move, but it turned out to be a very successful decision." Hugo joined Xiaomi to jump-start the exports to ten Asian countries, focusing on India.

Hugo told me that Xiaomi is different from a pure hardware company. "We think differently because we are software guys. We see the hardware as the delivery vehicle for our software." This is why Xiaomi is regarded as a contender for the "X title." According to a *Financial Times* interview with Xiaomi co-founder Bin Lin: "We see our main competition as the killer apps of the Chinese Internet: Tencent's WeChat, Alibaba's Taobao and Baidu." If Xiaomi hits its sales target in 2015, "Its total number of 'users' would be within striking distance of the top mobile apps in China," Bin Lin told the *Financial Times*.[30]

The reason Xiaomi can price its phone so affordably is that selling phones is not Xiaomi's aim; it is the means to an end. "We essentially price the hardware at cost and we put a small premium on the software. Most of the software revenues will come over time as opposed to at the time the person purchases the device. You can think of it as a platform more than anything else," Hugo told me. "Once the platform is in place, by developing software and applications we will start monetizing."

Having a big market capitalization is not enough to become the X. As JP was telling me, "To be the X you need to create your own market and ecosystem." This is why Xiaomi is pricing its phone so aggressively low. "As a software company, Xiaomi wants to position its software to do more things like enter into the smart home industry, for example," said Hugo.

The Internet of Things is indeed the ecosystem that JP was talking about and what could transform Xiaomi into a real Tech Titan. "IoT is not only appliances, but it is also software. Xiaomi is investing resources for the smart home of the future," said Hugo.

Finally, Hugo added, "Xiaomi is also an e-commerce company. When you log on to our flagship site, www.mi.com, you can see a full-on e-commerce website with thousands of SKUs, all of which are products that carry our brand and a minority are complementary products that work well with our phones and our hardware."

Yihaodian/Number One Store (Beijing)

Yihaodian, known in English as *Number One Store*, is a website that provides customers with a platform to shop for groceries and other goods. The company is famous for its forward-looking mindset.

Yihaodian operates a kind of virtual grocery store, in which images of grocery shelves are displayed on public surfaces. Shanghai and Beijing public transit commuters buy groceries with their phones, scanning QR codes on walls while they wait for their rides.

This concept of a virtual store, which Yihaodian pioneered, illustrates the O2O trend now taking China by storm. Shoppers who purchase in the morning find their groceries waiting at their doorstep by the time they return home in the evening. Not bad for a developing country. This was the opinion of retail giant Walmart, which took a majority stake in Yihaodian in 2011 and bought the entire company at the end of July 2015.

Flash Selling

"A 3.2 million Yuan [roughly 500,000 USD] roadster has been added to your shopping cart. You can now proceed to checkout."

This is what appeared before my eyes the first time I opened a flash sales website.

In June 2014, Glamoursales.com, also known as Mei.com, launched a joint campaign with Maserati to sell a Maserati Gran Cabrio Fendi limited-edition roadster.

They had my attention. I was curious to understand how an Italian supercar could be sold on a website. In developed markets, luxury brands are associated with VIP events and exclusive sporting competitions, like golf or sailing. Buying a luxury car means joining a club, sharing the same vision as your peers, and the luxury purchase experience.

Assuming I had the money, I was literally one click away from buying a supercar. But having the money is not enough to belong to the "club." Where was my experience in purchasing something so valuable? What happened to the exclusivity?

To better understand how the flash sales model works in China, I met with two experts: Michelangela Agnolin, an international business development director at VIP.com, and Thibault Villet, CEO and cofounder of Mei.com, which focuses on luxury products.

Listed on the NYSE since 2012, VIP.com is the Chinese flash sales market's major player. I visited their Shanghai office, on the 17th floor of a high-rise building towering above Chinese lane houses and a busy food market. A receptionist led me through a corridor lined with young Chinese workers looking at their screens and talking loudly on their phones. "This is our Shanghai customer service operation," said Michelangela as she greeted me, reading the curiosity in my eyes. Young and energetic, she walked me to her office at the end of the corridor and began explaining what makes VIP.com tick.

VIP.com profits by selling off-season, slow-moving products from other brands on its online channel. Each flash sales event lasts roughly five days, selling a limited number of items. Flash selling is considered to be a very efficient way to manage stock for brand owners who need or wish to clear their inventories. It is a win–win for both the merchant and for the websites handling the sale.[31]

To my surprise, flash sales companies do not fear mega platforms like Alibaba's Tmall or Taobao. "We focus on delivering a customer experience," explained Michelangela.

As intermediaries connecting customers to merchants, platforms are not usually responsible for delivery. Buyers can sometime wait for more than three days to receive a package. Three days in the West may seem acceptable, but is an eternity in China. "Chinese clients do not like to wait. Seeing a box being delivered makes the customer's eyes glitter. We ensure the fastest and most reliable delivery. This makes all the difference," said Michelangela.

Fast delivery is not VIP.com's only advantage. "When Chinese buyers purchase foreign brands for the first time, they sometimes find them too sophisticated. Often purchased out of curiosity to touch and see them, some products are later returned. This causes a higher return rate. Providing a sound return policy is key to developing a good customer base," Michelangela explained.

This customer-focused strategy reminded me of Primo chef Jacky's patience in changing dishes free of charge until customers are satisfied. It's the same principal Mei.com uses to develop consumer trust.

With offices located in a beautiful Victorian building at the heart of the Bund, Shanghai's old colonial concession, Mei.com is China's only successful non-Chinese flash sales site.

China is often painted as a graveyard for foreign Internet companies—Google pulled out, Facebook was shut out, Twitter was blocked. Recently, American Internet companies "Have found a degree of success in China . . . [by handing] over data and control to the Chinese government," writes Josh Horwitz in an article published in Quartz.[32] Mei.com shows, however, that even a foreign Internet company can really make it big in China when it has the right DNA and fits into the system—politics and data seem to have little to do with it.

Launched in Shanghai in 2009 by Thibault Villet, a seasoned veteran of luxury brands in Asia, Mei.com was first invested in 2012 by Neiman Marcus Group, the well-known U.S. retailer, for 28 million USD. Neiman sold its stake in 2014. At the same time, London-based asset management Investec and Hong Kong jewelry powerhouse Chow Tai Fook invested 65 million USD for an undisclosed amount. Finally, on July 8, Alibaba invested 100 million USD.

Mei.com profits by selling off-season, slow-moving products from top luxury brands such as Armani, Zegna or Michael Kors. Each flash sales event lasts roughly five days, selling a limited number of items. In 2014 the company sales exceeded 150 million USD, with over 2,400 brands sold on the platform.

Thibault believes that flash sales in China work not only with high-end, high-value luxury goods, but also with goods many Westerners wouldn't expect to find online. From Maserati to luxury yachts, almost anything can be bought through online flash sales.[33] "People love the convenience," he added. "At the moment, flash sales concentrate mainly on the products of luxury brands." But Thibault predicts that, "In the near future, we will see more luxury goods and holidays sold online in China."

The experience of buying luxury products in China can be quite different than in the West. No matter how expensive the object, in China promotions are still a critical sales driver. Affluent Chinese with the financial means to buy luxury products are the same people who are using the Internet and mobile apps like WeChat. This is quite different from Europe and the U.S. where the luxury audience is less inclined to shop online. Buying luxury goods on flash sales platforms is becoming mainstream in China and platforms have now achieved the same trustworthy status of bricks and mortar operations. This is why Alibaba has proven to be seriously interested in the growing flash sales market and placed its bet on Mei.com. Its reputation among brands and customers will benefit Alibaba's TMall growing image, as it is seriously committed to eliminate fakes from its platform and provide a true shopping experience. Furthermore, the partnership clearly shows that Mei.com's success is not the result of a lucky strike. On the contrary, the company has implemented a winning strategy based on three pillars—finding the right niche for China, having a very deep expertise and building a strong local team—which should be considered by all Internet companies, local or foreign, seeking to be acquired by a big Chinese platform.

For many foreign Internet businesses trying to break into the Chinese market, politics might certainly play its role; yet having a sound and successful business model is the first prerequisite and should not be underestimated. In the end, business is business.

May the Best Model Win

Currently China has two e-commerce models: the marketplace or "Ali model," and the direct sales system, known as the "JD model." Toine, Dining City's cofounder explained the difference in purchasing, using both models.

"Online purchasing is an emotional journey," Toine told me.[34] "As people expect to be entertained, their experience needs to be very good. Take, for example, Taobao, Alibaba's C2C (consumer to consumer) platform. It has a huge assortment and is very price-elastic, usually cheaper than other sites. As Chinese customers are very price sensitive, getting the best price is already a good start for an experience." But in Alibaba's marketplace model, the marketplace operator does not deliver goods; it is not blamed for delays or en-route damages. Nearly all problems bounce back to the vendor. "If you need to return the goods to a Taobao seller, once the money is released, it can become quite a challenging experience. You never know how fast it will ship and whether the product is still in stock." When a problem occurs, the purchasing experience is tarnished.

"Purchasing through direct sales is a different story," said Toine. The platform owns the goods and the logistics are integrated into the service. "The reason JD.com can stand shoulder to shoulder with

Alibaba's platforms is because it stands behind the products it sells and is willing to accept returns. It can deliver a consistent experience," explained Toine.

So, which e-commerce model is likely to prevail?

Current data show that marketplaces have a much larger market share than direct-sales platforms. But it is important to note that marketplaces have had more time to develop. On a recent trip to Hong Kong, I met with two seasoned managers who helped me gain a better understanding of the difference between the two models.

Junling Liu, Yihaodian's CEO, told me that it is hard to tell which model will prevail. "It is a big question and I do not know the answer yet. You need to have both because from the user experience perspective, one vendor can never satisfy the needs of all the consumers."

John Lindfors, who runs the Asian operations of global investment group Digital Sky Technologies or DST Global, a venture capital firm that counts Alibaba and JD.com as part of its Asian portfolio, explained his thoughts on the two models. "Looking at the two models, all the websites are now combining them. I do not think that one model will eventually overrule the other. The market is big enough for both models. They will sort of overlap in certain operations where they will be competing with each other."

Based on what Junling and John told me during our interviews, it is likely that both models will gradually become less polarized, perhaps converging towards a new model, one not yet defined.[35] What seems clear is that the battle between the two models will be fought over logistics and data.[36]

To ensure delivery in line with customer expectations, Alibaba is now moving into logistics, announcing a new delivery network in partnership with the Intime Group department store chain to invest 48 billion USD over five to eight years, bringing 24-hour delivery to 2,000 cities across China.[37] This type of partnership with existing logistics-services operators is different than JD.com's creation of a "fulfillment infrastructure" from scratch.

One of the reasons why large online direct sales companies have also begun adding their own marketplaces for independent vendors is Big Data.

Fan Fan, the Taobao and Tmall fashion entrepreneur, described the experience of being a small vendor using data. As she explained, platforms operating under the JD.com model are now adding marketplaces, which bring in more traffic, and therefore more data.

Thanks to data collection and analysis, businesses can boost sales by being more responsive. "Knowing what customers want allows you to build a new line of products more suitable to the client's taste and needs, in just a few days. This does not happen in a physical store where reaction time is much longer," Fan Fan noted.

Platforms are inserting themselves between customers and vendors. They have added a new link in the supply chain.

In the past, a tailor did everything himself: he met with customers, took their measurements, designed, sewed and adjusted the suits. The advent of China's new e-commerce platforms created an intermediate layer of vendors who do not produce, yet know exactly what their customers want.

Manufacturers and brand owners were once the experts on what their customers wanted. Now, platforms, and the intermediaries like Fan Fan operating on them, have become the experts. How? By collecting and analyzing more and more data.

The Ali and JD models seem to be converging to ensure both a consistent user experience and products that are more suitable to the new emerging consumer long tail. Customer segmentation in China is becoming more and more complex, so data play a key role in ensuring that the experience remains unique to every customer.

This brings us back to Violette and to what she has learned from her meetings with the digital marketing consultants helping her to build the company's e-commerce website. What is certain is that the entire Chinese e-commerce market will encounter fierce competition in the near future. Big players, such as Alibaba with Taobao and Tmall, JD.com, Yihaodian and others will gradually consolidate their platforms and improve their positions in the industry. As a consequence, it will be harder for smaller players to set up their individual e-commerce sites, and almost impossible for newcomers to enter this highly competitive market.

CHAPTER 4

Transformed Lives

Shelby 2013.10.24

On a hot June morning in Hangzhou, a white Porsche Cayenne S is parked near the small pedestrian alleys that make up the modern shopping district of Xihu Tian Di.

A model is posing inside the white car with light brown leather interior. The driver side door is open. She is wearing a pair of white sandals, a green dress, a pair of aviator glasses and a light brown

Havana hat. This is the photo shoot for the summer campaign of Greenlip, a Taobao fashion brand.

A little under 200 kilometers southwest of Shanghai, Hangzhou is both the capital and the largest city of the Zhejiang Province. One of the seven ancient capitals of China, Hangzhou is famous for its beautiful lake called West Lake. Situated at the lake's southern bank, Xihu Tian Di is a leisure destination embracing the deep history and culture of the city of Hangzhou.

Backed by the same group that developed Shanghai Xin Tian Di, Xihu Tian Di has become a new landmark in Hangzhou. It is an area filled with boutiques that sell international brands and up-market bars and restaurants that serve a variety of local flavors; it's a blend of nature and fashion.

It is the perfect location for a fashion campaign, especially since young women from Hangzhou love Greenlip, an online brand set up by Fan Fan and exclusively operating through Taobao and Tmall e-commerce platforms.

A resourceful 30-year-old Chinese entrepreneur, Fan Fan has created a small empire for herself selling apparel online. In 2013, she had revenues in excess of 80 million RMB, roughly 13 million USD.

Fan Fan's story shares features common among a new breed of Chinese Internet retail entrepreneurs called "Taobao Power Sellers." There are currently millions of them.

She grew up in a town 35 kilometers east of Hangzhou and was raised in a working class family. When she graduated from high school, Fan Fan asked to go to Hangzhou to attend university.

In 2003, while studying fashion design and tailoring, she opened her first Taobao shop at 20 years old. Her roommate had just opened a similar shop and was keen to introduce Fan Fan to the marketplace's opportunities. Initially Fan Fan didn't pay too much attention to her shop; instead she focused on her studies and her work as a model.

Soon, however, Fan Fan decided she wanted to become a fashion entrepreneur, but wasn't sure how to go about doing so. She had been hearing great things about Taobao for a few years so she finally decided to take it more seriously.

Armed with her intuition and fashion sense, Fan Fan went into the textile market in the city center and selected a few pieces of clothing to test the waters. She wanted to create a fashion campaign to generate interest in her shop, so she tapped into the experience she had from her modeling days and set up a photo shoot. She hired a photographer, chose the location, and even modeled the clothes herself. She posted everything on Taobao and waited.

Immediately she noticed that there was demand for precisely what she had purchased. Throughout her career, Fan Fan had learned how styling and presentation could transform even the most basic shirt into a coveted fashion item. She knew she could now use what she had learned to build a new type of business.

Soon customer demand exceeded Fan Fan's capacity. She traveled to the market frequently to purchase more clothes, but the local outlets were not organized enough to supply the thousands of pieces her customers wanted. This is when she had her breakthrough idea.

She decided to create her own line of clothing and launch a brand. She would use Western brands like Stella McCartney as inspiration but adapt the designs to suit her audience. They were sophisticated enough to want the look of designer clothes, but she needed to make them more affordable so that her young trend-driven customers could buy more often. She would then sell the clothes through her existing Taobao store, since she did not have the upfront capital needed to open a retail store.

Fan Fan soon met an online entrepreneur who offered to help expand her online presence and distinguish her site from the thousands of others on Taobao. They soon became business partners and created a Taobao brand called Greenlip.

Before launching the brand, Fan Fan and her partner had to solve one major problem: production. Fortunately, they discovered it was easier than they expected since Hangzhou is one of the world's most famous areas for apparel manufacturing. They could immediately access a huge supplier base at the most competitive prices.

They opened a showroom in one of the industrial areas of Hangzhou, which soon became their headquarters. They then selected a number of trusted suppliers who would produce the shoes, bags and clothing.

Fan Fan started promoting the line through fashion campaigns, which featured the types of models that young Chinese women identify with, shot in the kinds of locations that appeal most to her target market.

Greenlip was so successful that initially Fan Fan could not keep up with the demand. For two months Fan Fan rarely left her desk on the second floor of her showroom. She sent someone out twice a day to buy food that she would consume in front of her computer screen. She would wake up at 6 a.m. and work until 3 a.m. the next day. She would sleep and then start the process all over again.

By 2009, Taobao had turned into China's biggest and most successful e-commerce platform and its number of sellers had grown exponentially. Unfortunately, competition had also grown immensely and by that time the most successful sellers were copying each other. Fan Fan was losing her edge and Greenlip's revenues were slowing down.

Fan Fan needed to drive more people to her website. She had noticed that traffic peaked at the launch of a collection every month, but once the novelty wore off, customers drifted to other sites. Together with her suppliers she decided to launch weekly collections. That meant rotating her warehouse stock every week. She found herself running operations similar to the way global fast fashion names such as Li & Fung, Zara and H&M do.

The plan worked well initially, but once again competitors eventually caught up and began copying Fan Fan's business model. Again, she had to come up with a new idea.

A short-term measure was to open up more stores on Taobao and Tmall to differentiate the products. However, she knew that to support her growth in the long term she needed to find a new niche.

Through her customer feedback and friends she learned that pregnant women had very few options for fashionable maternity clothes. Fan Fan used her tailoring and design skills to create a new line of stylish maternity clothes. It was another hit and in 2013 reached a record high.

Fan Fan had finally found her new niche.

Power to the Individuals

As I reviewed my notes from Fan Fan's interview while riding the train back to Shanghai, I kept asking myself one question over and over again: *How did she do it?*

I have spent many years advising businesses on how best to establish and maintain profitable partnerships with local manufacturers in China. I have seen the sacrifices that successful local owners made to launch their business, purchase machinery, train staff and create sales channels from scratch.

I simply could not understand how a young person could become so successful without having to stump up capital, buy land, play the games and dance the dances that were a part of doing business in the days of China 2.0.

It seemed that everything that I had learned in the last ten years suddenly did not apply anymore. I was witnessing a new world that I was still struggling to understand.

My answer would arrive a few days later during an interview with an online jewelry business entrepreneur. She wished to remain anonymous in this book but agreed to share her story with me. I will call her Wang Jie.

Wang Jie is from Shanghai and she started her career in digital marketing working for a multinational company. Initially she was more focused on online magazines and blogs and then she moved over to social networks.

Several years later, one of her foreign clients was interested in opening an online business, and offered Wang Jie the job of opening their Tmall store.

She successfully opened the store and organized its sales force. When asked to open another new shop for the company, Wang Jie declined. She decided it was time to set up her own business, but in a very different sector: jewelry.

Around 100 kilometers west of Shanghai lies Suzhou. Often called "The Venice of the Orient," Suzhou is famous for its canals, silk production and pearls.

Wang Jie had noticed that the pearl market's supply chain had three main players: the manufacturers, the designers and the distributors. Each function was clearly separated and each player's cost was reflected in the pearls' final price.

She realized that pearl distribution was still very traditional, with wholesalers selling to physical stores. Furthermore, the jewelry designs did not reflect the taste of a new generation of young buyers. Wang Jie sensed an opportunity and approached the pearl market using Fan Fan's method.

She started designing necklaces and bracelets using some of the jewelry she saw in magazines as inspiration. She then selected the manufacturers for her line of jewelry. Finally, she launched her own brand.

With her background in marketing, she was knowledgeable about distribution channels. She started a blog on Weibo, China's famous

Twitter-like microblog, to educate her perspective customers on pearls and introduce them to her shop on Taobao.

She soon realized that while Taobao was a good advertising window, it was not the most effective way to reach her target audience. She catered to a more sophisticated crowd but was not yet ready to open a Tmall shop; its requirements were too high for her startup brand. This is when she got the idea to approach flash sales sites with her jewelry.

Flash sales sites target a different clientele than Taobao. They are focused on offering specific products and brands, curated for an audience of sophisticated young professionals like Violette, for a limited time, usually five to seven days. Flash sales sites allow business owners like Wang Jie to reach their target audience directly. This marketing phenomenon has turned Wang Jie into a very successful entrepreneur.

Contemplating Fan Fan's and Wang Jie's stories, I could not help wondering whether they were concerned about manufacturers bypassing them and opening Taobao stores of their own. After all, manufacturers had the production power, the finances and, most importantly, the designs.

To my surprise both answered: "Not at all." "Manufacturers are very good at producing," Wang Jie told me, "but it is not in their DNA to market and distribute and most of all to deal with the final customers. Most of them do not even know where to begin the process of opening an online store, use social networks and follow a flash sales campaign."

The reason Fan Fan and Wang Jie were not worried was because they were not competing against the manufacturers. Rather, they were actually taking work away from the distributors. With their hundreds of clients, Taobao sellers could source from suppliers and sell directly to customers, shortening the supply chain and eliminating the need for distributors.

Suddenly I found the answer to the *How do they do it?* question I had been asking myself since coming back from Hangzhou.

Thanks to the Internet and e-commerce platforms, people like Fan Fan and Wang Jie are now able to plug into the existing ecosystem of factories, workers and physical infrastructures and build a successful business on top of it. E-commerce platforms have in fact empowered individuals to carve out a niche for themselves between the producers and the customers and achieve their entrepreneurial dreams like never before.

By empowering individuals, e-commerce platforms are also fostering a new type of growth: bottom-up growth. Everyone now has the opportunity to make an economic impact on a national level because of the low entry barriers to the market. The infrastructure is already in place and is easily accessible. Fan Fan, Wang Jie and Taobao's millions of power sellers are living examples of this phenomenon. The entrepreneurial attitude of China has finally been unleashed.

This has both advantages and disadvantages. On the positive side, every hard working and ambitious individual can now launch an online business with limited resources. On the negative side, the low entry barriers are creating fierce competition and a lot of businesses are failing.

Opening a shop on Taobao has transformed Fan Fan's life. It has given her the opportunity to open her own business, which she could never have done without e-commerce.

E-commerce is not only bringing growth to China, it is also causing a social change, moving the paradigm from *power to the people*, to *power to the individuals*. For a country based on Communism and community values, this represents a huge change.

Before the Internet, Chinese people were viewed as extensions of the group they belonged to. Chinese society is based on families, communities, townships, regions and the Party. Even private factories are part of industrial zone communities. The Internet is now changing this very concept and empowering individuals to impact the economy on a much larger scale.

The Progress Is Online

On a Thursday night in August, I met Violette and her husband for a drink in the French Concession neighborhood of Shanghai. It was once an area of old lane houses, like the Shikumen houses of Xin Tian Di, and has recently been renovated to host restaurants, a florist and bars.

We met at a newly opened Australian wine bar. Wine is becoming very popular among the Chinese and wine bars have sprung up all over China's main cities, especially in the South. French, Italian,

Spanish, Australian and South American wines can now be found in most wine shops and online.

We sat outside and ordered a bottle of Merlot. The night was warm and we could still hear the crickets, even in the middle of the city.

Violette told me that her day went well and she was happy with the progress of her company's e-commerce site and new application. She had been quite busy because her grandfather was visiting from Taiwan.

She told me that he was an engineer who ran a factory in Nanjing, a city 300 kilometers northwest of Shanghai. I asked her to tell more about the China of her grandfather's time and to my surprise she told me a story that now sounded very familiar. Violette's husband smiled; he must have heard the story many times.

Violette's grandfather was head of a state-owned company that manufactured trucks. Originally the factory produced water pumps, but in the 1950s the government decided that it needed to create a truck and car industry to move people around China. Along with many others, her grandfather's factory was converted to a truck manufacturing plant.

I asked whether the workers, technicians and equipment were suitable to manufacturing trucks. Her answer was a resounding: "NO." Her grandfather's most difficult job was converting the factory. The equipment was not designed to manufacture trucks nor were the workers or technicians trained to assemble them. There was, however, the collective will to build the trucks. That was all they needed back then.

Determined, they modified existing equipment and built new machines better suited to their needs. Workers and engineers found a way to join two existing machines to manufacture the truck's chassis. Next, they built an experimental engine that initially lasted only a few thousand miles.

The engineers and workers made countless adjustments until they finally created a more reliable engine. The factory started producing trucks with the new engines that were soon deployed all over the region.

Violette's grandfather's story made me realize that in China, while many things remain constant, some things actually change.

The Internet and e-commerce in China were born in a very similar way to the truck manufacturing business of the 1950s. China knew that it needed to adopt the Internet to progress, but it had a limited understanding of how it worked. Its engineers were not as advanced as those who had developed the Internet in the West and in Japan. The Chinese studied U.S. companies like Google, Amazon and eBay, and worked through thousands of prototypes until they eventually created some of the biggest Internet conglomerates in the world.

However, there is a profound difference between what is happening today in China and what was happening in the 1950s. Back then, the government, as part of a five-year plan to build more vehicles and upgrade the transportation system in China, dictated the creation of the truck industry. Orders were coming from the top and state-owned factories created the new industry. In other words, it was a top-down approach.

Today one of the most important peculiarities of Chinese e-commerce is that innovation is being led by private entrepreneurship and individuals, rather than by government organizations. In other words, it is a bottom-up approach where individuals empowered by the Internet and e-commerce are now driving progress and reforms.

The government is setting very clear guidelines on where the market should be going and how it should be reformed, but it no longer intervenes. It follows an approach that in China is called *bu guan bu wen*, literally meaning "do not manage and do not ask." This approach means that there is no longer one centralized solution, but instead many disparate private solutions, which eventually consolidate into a market leader.

By moving the focus from top-down to bottom-up, China e-commerce has actually turned into a sustainable growth model that is not only transforming urban lives, but it is bringing progress to rural and developing areas, like the third and fourth tier cities.

Taobao, for example, has become increasingly important in boosting rural economies across China. Many villages now sell local handicrafts or local products on Taobao; they are the so-called Taobao Villages.

According to Alibaba's listing prospectus, a Taobao Village is any place where at least 10 percent of the population is engaged in online retailing. The prospectus claims that the phenomenon is growing fast, and that there are already 20 such villages across China, each generating at least 10 million RMB (or 1.6 million USD).

Setting up a Taobao shop has meant the freedom to work from home for many rural citizens instead of leaving in search of work in a construction site, or factory in a distant region of China. This can bring real change to people's lives in a country where every year millions of workers migrate looking for jobs.

One village, in the southern province of Guangdong, has taken the concept to the next level, opening a "Taobao University" where people come to learn how to sell online.

An article published in *The Economist* in June 2014[1] describes the village of Junpu and its local government, which is supporting Taobao sellers by providing free wireless Internet for residents, tax credits and "an informal plan to give free warehouse space to anyone who wants to keep inventory in the village."

The village used to host a low-tech food-processing industry. "Now, of the 3,000 residents in this tight-knit community, more than half make their living through Taobao," says the article. The village made the news not only in China but also in Africa and in the spring of 2014 a group of online retailers from Africa came to Junpu to study this phenomenon, and attended a three-week course at the local Taobao University.

This progress does not only mean that people from everywhere can access products, it also means that they can enjoy services even before traditional infrastructures to support them have been built in their areas.

China's lack of infrastructure has, in fact, turned out to be its biggest opportunity. To grow and prosper, BAT-X companies have created an entire online infrastructure to support e-commerce transactions. This structure is very similar to an ecosystem, made up of online payments, smart logistics and customer service applications that are penetrating China before physical infrastructures do.

In an interview released in the *Financial Times* right after China's Singles Day 2014, Joe Tsai, Alibaba's Executive Vice Chairman, said that rural China, where 9 percent of the population buys online compared with 30 percent in the cities, is now a priority for Alibaba. "When we see the rural opportunity we get very excited," he said.[2]

Chinese e-commerce has become so efficient that people now use it even in their "offline" life. BAT-X are now looking to transform antiquated state-dominated sectors such as financial services and health care, rolling out reforms to the current system. One of the biggest effects of these reforms will be felt in the remote parts of China.

One example can be found in the banking and finance sector. Mobile payments are not only disrupting the financial sector, but they are actually changing the lives of the people who live outside the developed cities.

Digital finance may reach people before banks do. Let's look at what it means for rural development to make financial services and insurance accessible by a mobile phone.

When Alibaba launched its online mutual fund Yuebao in 2013, it gave a rude awakening to China's banks. As the Shibor Index (the most important interest rate used in China's money market today) decreased, people moved their savings en masse into Yuebao, which paid a substantially higher rate.

Digital finance and mobile payments are not unique to China. Both Google and Apple have launched their own online payment systems, Google Wallet and Apple Pay, respectively. However, what makes China interesting is that mobile finance is leapfrogging the traditional financial system development.

Financial institutions have been operating in the U.S. for centuries, while China's traditional financial system continues to lag behind. The combination of Internet and widespread adoption of mobile technology now allows people in third and fourth tier cities in China to benefit from services such as mutual funds, insurance, and financial products that they could not access previously.

From Producer to Consumer in One Click

To learn more about reforms and efficiencies in the Chinese market brought about by e-commerce, I met with Junling Liu, CEO and co-founder of Yihaodian.

Also known in English as *The Number One Store*, it is a B2C (business to consumer) e-commerce platform, which allows customers to shop for groceries and many other goods. The retail giant Walmart now owns 100 percent of the company.

Among Yihaodian's many features, I believe two have had the biggest impact on China so far. The first is that it has given access to local and international food to everyone, with one simple click. The second is that it created a communication channel between producers and consumers. Buyers now know what they are eating.

Considering how serious the food safety issue is in China, what Yihaodian has achieved is remarkable. Junling shared with me how their revolutionary idea was born.

A former Vice President of Dell Inc., Junling and his business partner Gang Yu, Vice President of Dell's worldwide procurement, established Yihaodian in 2008 and it quickly became the number one store for online food purchasing in China.

"The idea of this platform was bouncing around in our heads for a while. When I was working with Dell, I was on the plane to Singapore once a month and had a lot of time to think; that is when the idea came. Ever since, I could not sleep. Back then my partner and I did not know what we were getting ourselves into," said Junling laughing.

"It was the right time to do it, but when we launched the business in July 2008, we were not lucky because the investment community had dried up; no one knew how bad the recession was going to be and whether we could get funding. Then we made it and people were suddenly queuing up to write checks to us when we no longer needed the money. We worked very hard to survive during those times.

"Launching a food platform from scratch was challenging. But the best part was that I enjoyed the experience to transform myself from multinational executive into entrepreneur. Nothing can beat that reward," he told me.

Junling's humbleness is what impressed me the most about him. Yihaodian is by far one of the most successful e-commerce platforms in China; yet when talking about the company's beginnings, Junling is the living example of the Chinese proverb: "modesty fortifies, arrogance weakens." "During my transformation I encountered some personal limits," he recalled. "For example, I did not know how to book a plane ticket. I had to learn how to use the subway to travel around Shanghai and I had never done it before. I did not know where to recruit people. I had to learn how to advertise our company and how to write a software code.

"At the beginning we thought we knew a lot, but customers were not responding the way we wanted. For example, we distributed catalogues because we thought it was what customers wanted, but it turned out to be wrong. We had to learn quickly about our limitations and also our strengths."

Like any startup, Yihaodian's biggest challenge during its first year was attracting customers. "It took us a whole year to get to a critical mass. First, we had 20 orders from internal staff and then it took us a whole year to get to 1,000," said Junling. "The question was always the same: *How do we get our customers to know who Yihaodian is and what we do?*"

They had to find an inexpensive way to spread the word about their new company. "When you do not have money you have to carefully choose the channels and the ways, like word of mouth, etc.," Junling explained. The hard work paid off; 12 months after the company started it hit 1,000 orders in one day. "That was a crucial milestone and we had a huge celebration," said Junling. "It takes 1,000 orders to test every corner of your operations. Before that, you do not know the limitations of your operations and the overall experience: sourcing, warehousing, picking, user experience and your system. You do not know where the crisis is going to come from."

Indeed, Yihaodian has achieved something truly unique for China, and has brought real change to people's lives. Thanks to e-commerce platforms like Yihaodian, every person from the urban Beijingnese to rural fourth tier residents, now has access to most of the products available nationwide. Considering that China never had national chains like Walmart or Costco in the U.S., China e-commerce has achieved the same result with a much more limited expenditure.

Local products are not the only things Chinese are now shopping for. Online platforms are increasing the assortment of imported and packaged food available to Chinese consumers at competitive prices.

"In the past China was heavily export driven; now the government wants to balance trade by increasing imports," said Junling. "If you look at our imported food category, the growth is actually faster than that of the local food. That sends you a message: Chinese people are curious about products from outside China. We have discovered that customers want to try something new and in our case we allow our customers to travel virtually to countries around the world enjoying 'cousins' from the Mediterranean, United States, Australia, South East Asia, etc. We are able to source products and bring them to customers without them having to ever leave their houses."

Given ongoing food safety issues, online platforms have become alternative channels for purchasing imported and packaged food, which ensures a greater selection.

I checked Yihaodian to see what types of imported food could be purchased. When you log on, the website firsts asks you where you are located. I tried entering different cities and in most of the places

I found the same products at similar prices. This is something that was nearly impossible in China prior to 2008.

I recall that before 2012 it was difficult to find high-quality imported products at reasonable prices in China. When I went home to Italy, I would fill my suitcase with products such as olive oil or balsamic vinegar. Fast forward two years, and not only can you find them online in China, but people living in less developed areas of the country are able to buy the same quality olive oil and balsamic vinegar at similar prices to those found in Beijing, Canton or Shanghai. This progress is coming from these online platforms.

Yihaodian does not only sell products using the direct sales model, it also hosts a marketplace. Third parties can sell their own products to the very same customers that are shopping on Yihaodian. For example, a coffee producer in Yunnan, a famous region in the southwest part of China bordering Vietnam, Laos and Myanmar can now sell its coffee to pretty much every city in China without a physical store or a wholesaler.

This has tremendous impact both on farmers and on consumers. "E-commerce is helping farmers to sell better and this is just the beginning," said Junling. "Currently, there are simply too many layers between a farmer and, for example, the Carrefour's shelves. The supply chain, from my perspective, is tremendously long and wasteful. By the time it hits the shelves, a 10 yuan product for example could now cost 15 yuan. We are making an attempt to connect the farmers with the consumers directly. It is a win–win strategy."

"When you look at our marketplace, we already have suppliers that are literally going to the field digging the veggies for customers who have just ordered them. It cannot get fresher than this. In the future we will be able to use the platform to provide customers with real time information such as where the product is grown, how reliable it is and who is going to stand behind the product's quality. We can actually show the customers how it is produced, and from which farm exactly. Customers can even say that they want to buy that specific apple tree, for example. That opens up tremendous possibilities. There is true value that is going to be created in that effort," Junling explained.

According to a report by Morgan Stanley[3]: "Online marketplaces are increasing customer to business products and services in various sub-sectors, including fresh food . . . This model is especially effective for seasonal products that can be sourced in large quantities like fruit and seafood . . . Products are advertised online and/or offline to receive orders before production/harvesting."

By opening a channel between consumers and producers, platforms can anticipate consumers' needs and optimize production.

The advantage is not only economic. By not having to deal with so many layers, farmers can now reach the customer directly, interact with them and even create their own brands. Once again, bottom-up growth.

"Thanks to the Internet and e-commerce, we are experiencing a tremendous change in the relationship between producers and final users," said Junling. "A farmer can now say: 'Mr Customer, I am ABC veggie grower and I want you to be my loyal customer, I will give you this and this product especially grown for you.' Whereas, in the past farmers did not know who their customers were. I see a lot of value in that," said Junling.

After listening to Fan Fan, Wang Jie and Junling, I realized that for developed countries, e-commerce might be a new way to do something old. But for the developing world like China, it is the obvious way to do something new. This is why China e-commerce is not only a commercial model, but also a new model for growth.

CHAPTER 5

A Super-Connected World

Four great cities representing the world's rising economy, Beijing, San Francisco, Bangalore and Tokyo, host the Global Mobile Internet Conference (GMIC). Each year at GMIC, tens of thousands of executives, entrepreneurs and investors from around the globe meet for three days and build the partnerships now transforming the way we shop, communicate and entertain ourselves.

These architects of our future flock to the Olympic Village, across from Beijing's 2008 Olympic monument, Bird's Nest Stadium. Eager to discover the newest applications, online games and smartphones, they fill the streets and the magnificent halls of China's National Convention Center.

The May air is crisp, the sky is blue and the sun is shining. Dark, polluted skies seem far away. Colorful flags everywhere add to the sense of innovation and excitement. You can almost touch it.

Beijing GMIC is now Asia's single largest mobile conference. In one room on the Convention Center's second floor, Tencent CEO Pony Ma is explaining the connections his company has successfully created between people. The next frontier will be connecting everything else to the Internet—the so-called Internet of Things.

Next door, one of the Center's largest rooms is filled with hundreds of young Chinese entrepreneurs, there for an event called G-Startup. Twenty startups from around the world serve their pitches to a panel of experts. The winning team will get financing and coaching from successful founders and investors.

The stage can barely hold all the participants. Among them is Bruce Nikoo, excited to introduce his online-to-offline (O2O) application Kaado to the judges and attendees. He stands by a window gazing at the stadium as he gathers his thoughts.

Designed by the Swiss architecture firm Herzog & de Meuron, Bird's Nest Stadium combines Chinese tradition and modernity. Its design includes the traditional element of Chinese ceramics, while modern steel beams wrap the building and give it the appearance of a bird's nest.

Bruce's eyes trace the stadium's intricate patterns as he reflects on the early lessons on construction he learned from his father that launched his journey to GMIC.

Born in Tehran to a Persian mother and a father of Russian origin, Bruce was introduced to entrepreneurship and commerce at a young age. His father, once a banking executive, branched out on his own, setting up a business trading construction materials and building houses. Bruce earned degrees in Mechanical Engineering and Communications Systems Management, but remained fascinated with international trade. After graduating, he moved to Dubai to help manage his father's business affairs across the Middle East and from Russia to Canada. This led him to Toronto, where he worked with the Ministry of International Trade assisting foreign investor delegations wanting to explore Canada's investment opportunities.

While in Toronto, Bruce became more interested in IT. He took IBM courses in Product and Project Management and learned to develop Web-based products. It was 2004, Web-based companies such as Google and Apple were expanding and Facebook was just born.

Each month, Bruce would rush to the newsstand and purchase the latest copy of *Business 2.0*. He would study each issue, learning the ins and outs of the evolving tech industry. The magazine covered the early tech boom in the late 1990s, then the bust, followed by the phoenix-like rise of the modern Web in the early 2000s when websites were little more than information pages. Then came the rise of Facebook, when websites became interactive and applications began to appear.

Bruce was strongly influenced by three of the magazine's "10 Driving Principles of the New Economy," from its 1998 inaugural issue: space, market and impulse. *Business 2.0* promised that distance between buyers and sellers would soon vanish. Buyers would gain power while sellers would gain new opportunities. Ultimately every product would be available almost anywhere. These were the seeds of what Bruce would later envision for Kaado.

In 2007, Apple launched the iPhone. Sooner than many, Bruce realized the tech world had just changed, seeing immediately that the mobile phone would become the best device to reach people and provide information—far better than the PC.

A friend's introduction led Bruce to a job as a web product manager, developing products that included Canada's first Internet televisions (IPTV) services. In 2010, he traveled to South Korea and China looking for suppliers for the IPTV set-top box, or decoder. It was during that trip that he fell in love with China.

Bruce had read about China's early tech scene in books like *Silicon Dragon* and other Western publications and blogs. Once there, he saw that it was even more dynamic than he had initially realized. He began visiting China regularly, and on one of those trips encountered a Finland-based cross-border e-commerce company.

The company was looking for candidates to enter the Chinese e-commerce market. At the end of 2011, Bruce offered to partner with them and open their Beijing office. A few months later, Bruce was on Finnair flight AY31 bound for Helsinki to attend a board meeting where he would propose his plan. The meeting went well and Bruce went back to Toronto, resigned amicably from his job, and packed for Beijing.

At last, Bruce was on the brink of becoming an entrepreneur, but the excitement was short-lived. China had become much more expensive than just a few years before and his Finnish partners balked at the idea of committing so many resources to one country and scrapped the plans for a Beijing office.

By spring 2012, Bruce was alone in Beijing, unemployed and unsure of what to do next. He wanted to become an entrepreneur in China's fast-growing tech industry, but did not know how to start and run a company in China. He loved challenges, but this was a big bone to chew. He was in a huge country struggling to communicate—at that time very few people spoke English, even in the tech world.

Bruce's years of living internationally, from Tehran to Dubai to Toronto, taught him: when in Rome, do as the Romans do. To survive in China, he knew he needed to embrace the local language and culture. Suddenly, age 40, he found himself back in a classroom studying elementary Chinese.

Learning the language was critical to the next step in embracing the culture: networking. He even picked a Chinese name: *Ni Bao Ran*. His university teacher's words echoed in his mind: "Wherever you go in the world, network, network, network until you drop dead." So he networked and observed.

Soon, he began to realize what was happening around him. His friends and classmates were living on their mobiles, looking at their screens before going to sleep and again as soon as they woke up. They were going online to shop for themselves and to buy gifts for one another. This gave Bruce his idea for Kaado.

In April 2012, Bruce pitched his concept to 30 people. He wanted to create an application to allow retailers and brands to offer digital gift cards to consumers. This would drive people into stores and increase sales.

In other words, he wanted to connect the digital and the physical worlds.

He used his iPad to create a mock-up and circulated it in search of a partner. Eventually he was introduced to an angel investor and after three months of discussion, they started the business together.

By the end of 2012, Bruce and his partner had accomplished a lot. They had rented an office in Beijing, registered the company, hired staff and developed the beta version of the application, which shipped a mere ten months later, right before China's October national holidays. An updated version had launched just a few days before GMIC and now his partner was sitting proudly in the amphitheater waiting for Bruce to officially present it.

When the Chinese government commissioned the Bird's Nest Stadium, they decreed it had to be a vessel for the people. Bruce was now conveying the same message: his application was the vessel connecting two worlds, the online and the offline.

The Wall Has Fallen

I attended the 2014 Beijing GMIC to learn about China's mobile industry and its market of about 1.3 billion subscriptions—more than six times the population of Brazil.[1] Were I writing this story in 2013, smartphones would have been an important, but not central, part of the story. My generation grew up surfing the Internet with desktops and laptops. For hundreds of millions of Chinese, however, mobile is their only tool to go online. In 2013, the number of active smart devices grew from 380 million to 700 million.[2] In just 12 months the Chinese leapfrogged PCs and went directly to smartphones. Almost 90 percent of Chinese citizens are now accessing the Internet using a mobile phone.[3]

Suddenly it is a different world.

In 2013, when I attended Singularity University, the transformative role of smart devices was a central topic of discussion. We theorized that in 2033 there would be no PCs. Mark Pincus, CEO of mobile game giant Zynga, told us users had migrated en masse to mobile devices.

"Smart devices will have their biggest impact when applications are developed mobile for mobile," Krzysztof, the tech investment banker with China Renaissance Partners, told me in Hong Kong. "Mobile services are still conceived with the desktop in mind. Web pages are simply resized to fit smaller screens and websites are turned into applications. Though they are growing rapidly, revenues from mobile are still quite small. Mobile has not yet expressed its full potential."

It was not until the Beijing GMIC that I understood where smart devices would make their biggest impact and on an unprecedented scale: China. After meeting Bruce at G-Startup, I knew I was looking at an entirely new world.

"China is going to become a super-connected world," Bruce predicted. "In China, mobile phones have linked the digital to the physical world and made it one. This is happening because digital has developed faster. Now it is making the physical world better." Bruce calls this the "phygital world."

Bruce and his application Kaado are taking advantage of this new phygital world. The application gives a glimpse into what the connected world will look like. To attract customers, shops create promotions using digital gift cards. Kaado sends these cards to users and drives potential customers into physical stores. Customers can use the card to collect an item or to discount a more expensive one. The gift card works as a motivator to shop and improves offline sales. It's a win–win for both retailers and customers.

"Chinese consumers shop in a unique way," Bruce explained. "A new generation of shoppers is demanding that retailers provide a more converged experience connecting their digital and physical worlds. They want to shop in a world with no boundaries and have access to any product, anywhere. Mobile phones are better than laptops because they can provide information specific to a person's location." The wall between the two worlds has fallen.[4]

The Chinese service industry is the biggest example of a world seen through a mobile screen. "It is where smartphones make their biggest impact," Bruce told me. Services have become social, local and mobile—better known as SO-LO-MO.

Kaado is part of a category of applications that grease the wheels of O2O commerce. Bruce explained how this concept of O2O works: "You walk around with your smartphone in your hand. The physical world is around you and the digital world on your screen. Your phone is the zipper holding the two worlds together."

O2O is booming, particularly in China. Thanks to a growing and stabilizing economy, young Chinese consumers' disposable income and their confidence in spending are increasing. They are choosing to spend their money on categories that improve their lifestyle and they are doing it locally. As retailers and restaurants struggle to bring traffic into their stores, smartphones have found a way to drive traffic, as Kaado demonstrates. "This trend is already happening and it is going to become a new lifestyle," Bruce predicted.

"Ten years from now, we will be living in cities where people and most of the things around them are pretty much connected wherever they go. Everything will be on-grid. People will give up their PCs and laptops and use their phone as mini computers," said Bruce. "I do everything on my phone. Though the screen is small, I still manage to get almost everything done."

"What I really need is the Internet. That's all. I order my food on my way home and it is delivered as I enter my building. Not long from now, refrigerators connected to the Internet will make orders for you or send a message informing you that you have to buy milk."

"The Internet of Everything" is just around the corner and soon will penetrate many people's lives. "Applications that can offer more added value between our lifestyles and all these connected things will become the killer app," Bruce insisted. Applications like Kaado will change the way we use services. As Tencent's Pony Ma told a nearby crowd while Bruce waited to address the G-Startup session, "Everything will be connected in a seamless world."

* * *

Violette gathers her notes from the wood-and-metal table, and looks out at the city of Shanghai through the tall glass window. A refreshing wind has cleared the air and provided good visibility of the city with its 20 million inhabitants.

Violette enjoys going to the Shanghai World Financial Center for meetings with her digital marketing agency. With its bottle-opener shape, it is one of the tallest buildings in the city.

Today's meeting was informative and somewhat alarming. In addition to the company's e-commerce site, Violette's team is also developing a new application, which she has just learned does not take full advantage of mobile's capabilities.

To give Violette an example of an O2O application, the agency showed her a service they recently developed for one of their clients, Yihaodian. Billboards of the client's products and QR codes were placed at several MTR (Mass Transit Railway) stops. Using their smartphones to scan the codes, people shopped while waiting for their rides.

Violette's company does not have an O2O strategy at the moment. The dotcom offices are not even in the same building as the other departments. She realizes that if the online and offline teams do not coordinate, it could lead to problems. She knows she needs to bring this to the attention of the two teams when she gets back to her office.

After the meeting, Violette takes two elevators down to the lobby and is finally outside. Her thoughts turn to her plans for the evening.

She remembers that her parents are visiting for dinner and she has promised to cook.

Violette has time to stop by the supermarket on her way back to the office but does not want to carry the bags. She could shop online, of course, but today she is in the mood to do something different.

Her assistant, Wang Wang, recently told her about online grocery chain Yihaodian's brilliant concept: 3D virtual department stores positioned throughout Shanghai's main commercial areas.

Violette takes out her mobile phone and opens the Yihaodian application to look for a store in the neighborhood. A flashing arrow guides her to a park entrance a few hundred meters away. To the naked eye, she is looking at a patch of grass, but when she looks at her phone, that grass has been transformed into a fully stocked 3D virtual supermarket. It feels like a video game.

Violette browses the digital aisles stocked with food and beverages. She scans a few cases of Evian water and a bottle of Argentinean Malbec. It is on promotion—discount coupons are placed throughout the virtual store—and she wants her parents to try it.

When she finishes her shopping, she goes to her virtual basket, checks out and selects the delivery time: 7 p.m., right on time for dinner preparations.

"While traditional Chinese stores began to offer online shopping, Yihaodian came from the opposite direction to create something entirely fresh and new," explained Junling, Yihaodian's CEO. "Our message is that e-commerce companies can also open physical stores. Technology-wise you can use the GPS to open a store in just a few seconds."

In the face of this fast-growing trend, will physical stores be able to resist the Internet's disruptive force? I met with an expert in consumer markets and technology to understand more. Erica Poon Werkun heads Consumer and Internet Research for UBS Securities Asia in Hong Kong and is very knowledgeable about O2O. "Physical stores will not completely disappear. People still need to touch things, open them up, and check them out. It is part of the shopping culture," she explained.

Erica expects a significant consolidation in the retail industry. Many shops will turn into "showcases" while others will eventually close. China's O2O will become a new way to shop, but it still needs to solve the price-leveling issue.

"The matching of online and offline prices is a difficult task which is bound to happen gradually," Erica explained. "First, prices will become more uniform among online players given the high level of transparency. Then, offline stores will try to match the online prices, although this is not an easy task. Finally, we may see more price matching among offline stores due to more transparency enabled by the Internet."

What is certain is that China's O2O trend seems to be here to stay. In a country that is still commercially underdeveloped, retail growth in bricks-and-mortar stores is being outpaced by O2O, and the gap between the two is bound to get wider.

The Ecosystem

Although O2O is a worldwide phenomenon, China has once again developed its own unique approach to an existing trend. "It is funny because O2O is a term that was coined in the U.S. but never stuck there, whereas it really took off here," says Kaiser Kuo, Baidu's director for international communications. "In the past, when I talked to journalists using the term O2O, some of them called it a very good way to define the combination of the digital and physical world, showing that the term O2O was not really used in the U.S."

Rather than the American model, led by traditional "big box" retailers that offer "click-and-pick"—online purchase followed by off-line pickup—China's "BAT-X" (Baidu, Alibaba, Tencent and the X) companies have pioneered something entirely different. Kaiser believes that: "2014 and 2015 have seen a very big development in O2O. The innovative model that we are developing in China is the biggest difference between the Internet that we are building here and what you currently see in other parts of the world. No one can say that China is still copying. We are inventing something radically different. We are witnessing a macro shift between a consumption-based growth in favor of services lead growth and O2O is a big part of this rebalancing. It is very fascinating."

China's O2O model is different because the environment where it is developing is different. China doesn't have mammoth chains comparable to the U.S.'s Walmart, Britain's Tesco or France's Carrefour, which are big enough to set up their own e-commerce platforms. Its smaller offline retailers need the Internet companies' consumer base and technological infrastructure to reach scale.

"Let's pick, for example, hotels," says Kaiser. "Most of the time when people travel in the U.S. they stay at hotel chains. They are often nationals or regionals: Howard Johnson, Holiday Inn, Days Inn. These companies have a large national back office staff doing national advertising and managing online reservations. That is not the case with China's hotel industry, which is actually very fragmented. There are a few chains, but most hotels are family or small companies. They do not have an online presence and it is not economical for them to buy advertising, for example, on Baidu. They need somebody to aggregate and provide the infrastructure for them. The same happens with restaurants. They do not have that back office staff that is able to build for them. It is the backwardness of Chinese infrastructures that is allowing O2O to develop in this way.

China's underdeveloped retail landscape provided a unique opportunity for Internet companies and applications like Kaado.

"Once again China has turned a weakness into an opportunity," Krzysztof, the tech investment banker, told me. "In China there are many more offline inefficiencies than in the U.S. Therefore, the efficiency gains for Internet companies are much bigger."

How did Internet firms like Alibaba avoid the obstacles that plagued China's bricks-and-mortar stores? By creating their own infrastructures, e-commerce ecosystems that incorporated logistics and national payment systems.

Inconsistent regulation—localities often squeeze revenue from their control of transportation—had made domestic shipping prohibitively expensive and confined most traditional retailers to their own regions.[5] The rise of online purchasing allowed retailers to bypass these barriers and reach consumers more efficiently.

Kaado illustrates this trend. When Bruce studied the gift-buying industry, he realized that, unless you go in person or send a courier, there was no easy way to deliver goods. Since Chinese cities are large and congested, he thought he could build a virtual delivery service using mobile phones. When in Rome, do as the Romans do.

Payments were another issue. Alibaba's Alipay and Tencent's TenPay platforms offered consumers a safer method for buying from strangers. These online platforms quickly replaced credit and debit cards as the preferred method of payment in China.

The infrastructure created by Internet companies quickly became a better alternative to the offline infrastructures. This further strengthened the link between the digital and physical worlds, and is the key reason why Internet companies lead O2O in China.

The e-commerce infrastructure is not limited to logistics and payments. It has expanded to every aspect of commerce from finance to health care and even to transportation.

Taxi applications such as Tencent's Didi Dache, Alibaba's Kuaidi Dache and Baidu's investment in Uber are all examples.[6] Since these services launched, it is no longer necessary to try to hail a taxi at rush hour. Instead of stopping for outstretched arms, drivers are now responding to mobile users. Booking a taxi has become more convenient for everyone, and also less expensive. Riders are incentivized with rebates; drivers with tips. Welcome to the super-connected world of O2O.

In February 2015 Didi Dache and Kuaidi merged creating Didi-Kuaidi, one of the world's largest smartphone-based transport services valued at around 8.8 billion USD.[7] To better understand the taxi application's booming sector, I sat down with Dexter Lu, CEO and founder of Kuaidi Dache and now joint CEO of Didi-Kuaidi. Originally from Hangzhou, Alibaba's hometown, Dexter moved to Texas in the mid-1990s to pursue a Master's Degree in Computer Science as well as an MBA. Initially working as a coder, he later became a product manager for an engineering company, splitting his time between Dallas and Silicon Valley.

Dexter traveled back to China in 2004 where great opportunities awaited him. In 2006, he launched his first business in Shanghai, an SMS-based social network similar to Dodgeball, a U.S. location-based social network, which notified you about which of your friends were in your proximity. The business did not do well because smartphones did not exist yet. "All of the phones were feature phones and the user experience was terrible," said Dexter. That was, however, a good opportunity for him to learn about the so-called mobile Internet world. When the iPhone arrived in 2007, just like what Bruce had realized, Dexter knew that he finally had the right tool in hand for his new idea.

While traveling inside China, Dexter realized that catching a taxi during certain hours was very difficult. For example, during evening shifts, when taxi drivers break for dinner, "finding a cab in Hangzhou was like winning the lottery," he said. "I wanted to find a solution."

He assembled a small team and started his business in 2012 in Hangzhou, his hometown. "I did not really think that we could become so big. During that time we just wanted to solve a problem," said Dexter.

The beginning was difficult. "Logically, we started by approaching the city's main taxi companies, but they did not take us seriously. Taxi companies are state-owned enterprises and do not really talk to young entrepreneurs."

Dexter turned his attention to a successful London taxi application called Hailo. "I saw something there that could work in China," he said. Looking deeper into Hailo's model, Dexter realized that he had approached the wrong audience. To succeed, he needed to talk to the taxi drivers directly.

"It was not our plan to be like Hailo; we just found their model well suited to the Chinese market," Dexter explained. "We set up our operations team and started working with the drivers. They were very smart, and knew this would help their business, especially during those periods when they did not have customers."

Before Didi and Kuaidi merged, I asked Dexter why there were only three major taxi applications left in China—Didi, Kuaidi and Uber. "Until 2013, you had ten to 12 applications and then only a few remained. You need a very strong team and very deep pockets. The teams that have survived are the best fitted for this race," he explained. Eventually, Didi and Kuaidi merged because their unprecedented cash-burning race and the subsidies that they were paying to taxi companies could not last forever. As a result, you now see taxi drivers with two to three smartphones in front of them with all of the competing applications open so they can choose which one to respond to. As Dexter was telling me, drivers have become much more independent in managing their rides. This proves how disruptive the Internet can be even in a highly regulated country like China.

Taxi applications are another example of how platforms use different O2O strategies to attract passengers. Tencent and Alibaba are betting that users prefer to access services while networking on WeChat or doing shopping, and Baidu thinks that users will search for a taxi while looking for directions, thus integrating the on-demand car service into its maps service, giving Uber an audience of about half a billion.

"BAT companies use very different strategies to attract customers to their ecosystems," says Sharon Ng, Head of Investor Relations for Baidu. During our meeting in Beijing Sharon carefully explained to me how Baidu attracts traffic. "All Internet companies see that there is a very large opportunity in O2O and everyone is trying to figure out how to participate in O2O, but the degree of involvement and the degree of investment are very different across platforms. Therefore, the starting point why users should discover O2O with Baidu, Tencent or Alibaba is also definitely very different. So, for example, when users are on the Baidu application, they come to our box whether it is to search or for maps. By doing this every day they tell us what they are looking for. That puts Baidu in a very advantageous position since we learn what they are looking for. If you, as the box, continue to give users the shortest path to what they are looking for, they are going to keep coming back to you. Advertisers and marketers want to be there too. What more powerful position can that be when somebody is telling you what they want and you are right there when they are asking for it?"

Listening to Sharon describing to me how each BAT-X provides a different user experience makes me think that the platforms "war" happening in China is like seeing Facebook battling against PayPal and Google Maps. Alibaba and Tencent replicate their alternate strategies each time they add a new O2O function to their ecosystem, in areas such as financial services. Alibaba's Alipay-based Yuebao, meaning "save what's left," has become one of the world's biggest money-market funds. When people use Alipay to purchase or receive payments, they can directly invest their earnings in an interest-bearing account.

Because of its size, traditional banks are beginning to view Yuebao, with its higher returns and elimination of fees and minimums, as a real disruption. Tencent and Baidu also offer money-market accounts.

The opportunity Internet companies are now seizing—to create and develop unique ecosystems for finance, travel, health care and beyond—is a direct consequence of China's immature market economy. The period between the phase-out of central planning and the growth of the Internet was not enough time for traditional Western-style corporations to take root.

In Jack Ma's words, while American consumers "see e-commerce as dessert," China's traditional commercial infrastructure is so poor that "e-commerce becomes the main course."

The O2O models of China's tech companies are now poised to disrupt seemingly any industry. Entire industry verticals will move online, thanks to smart devices.

The Models

The emergence of this super-connected world, and the fierce competition among Chinese Internet companies to develop better solutions, makes it more likely that the next O2O revolution will come from China.

Online payments systems for the offline world are clear examples of China's advantage over the West. Each BAT-X company is developing its own payment system fueling a competition that will eventually create a better and more efficient super system that will be used by hundreds of millions of people. This new system will likely be more advanced than those in the West, which cater to a much smaller audience. This is yet another example of a revolution brought about by evolution.

"We've already experienced cashless payment and now cardless payment systems are coming in with a roar. The seamless experience of paying online and offline using the same tool will happen very fast," explained Bruce, Kaado's inventor. When he goes to Dairy Queen in Beijing, he uses TenPay, the WeChat payment system. Credit cards and cash payments will be completely replaced by online payments; bricks-and-mortar stores and consumers will converge online.

The new online payment platforms show how an O2O instrument can push Internet companies to enter industries previously dominated by offline corporations. The pre-existing industry has to reform itself or otherwise succumb. This is what drives mass-scale innovation in China.

"I use Alipay or TenPay to pay for taxis," Bruce told me. "I use them all the time and some taxis even offer in-car Wi-Fi to make it easier for me to make a mobile payment. While this is widely used in big cities in China, it's still not that common in many cities in North America or Europe where online shopping is popular but not to the level it is in China."

Tech habits are embedded in the culture. As Bruce explained, "For example, people in China use emails far less than they use instant messaging services like QQ and WeChat, even for business communications. The same happens when using online payment systems versus credit cards."

New payment systems are constantly developed for the Chinese market, by both Chinese and Western companies: in September 2014,

Apple launched Apple Pay, whose ability to compete with Chinese popular online and mobile payment systems has yet to be tested.

Chinese payment systems and O2O systems are likely to find fertile ground in countries where poor infrastructure creates space for technology to improve the offline sector.

QR codes are another example of China's successful evolutionary innovation in retail. Developed a decade ago in Japan, they are quickly catching on in China. A 2014 report by Morgan Stanley[8] expects QR codes to ". . . transform China into a multi-touch-point retail environment" and free shopping from its physical constraints. This is in contrast to a Bluetooth-based platform like Beacon that increasingly connects Western retailers to consumers via mobile devices. QR codes, which Violette used to get discounts at the Yihaodian virtual supermarket, will "offer the entire retail value chain from data analytics, traceability, display, to engagement and conversion," according to the report.

From Brokers to Principals

Beginning with simple e-commerce marketplace platforms Internet companies have now moved into every sector related to commerce. They have improved existing services, invented new ones and brought services to areas where previously there were none.

In retail, these new platforms are connecting the local offline supermarkets and store chains to buyers across China's vast expanse. In finance, they are creating money market funds and retail products people can use anywhere in the country—without ever going to a bank. In health care, they are connecting hospitals and doctors to patients living in villages and remote areas.

By carving out a middle role for themselves, they have become an integral part of the worlds to which they are the gatekeepers. In fact, Chinese tech companies have gone from simply connectors of the online and offline worlds to the leaders of O2O's world itself: from brokers to principals.

It's interesting to see how different this is from the U.S., where retail chains, hospitals and banks moved online, creating their own platforms, hardly partnering with tech companies except as back-end vendors. For hundreds of millions of people in China, e-commerce and its services are just "commerce," pure and simple.

What does this mean for China? There will be enormous opportunity for the Internet sector, especially in administering and improving services. Since each service carries user data, administering the system means providing data to the offline world that it could never gather by itself.

When Bruce created Kaado, he understood that connecting the two worlds would also bring a fundamental advantage: client profiling. No offline retailer could gather such sophisticated information on every buyer who enters its shops so quickly and affordably, and on such a large scale.

Thanks to mobile technology, Kaado and the other O2O applications are now able to provide intelligence as well as services. Across many industries, this intelligence is like a sophisticated navigation tool. Once, only the largest brands could afford to collect this kind of information on their customers; now each bricks-and-mortar operation has access to the data.

Kaiser and Sharon from Baidu gave me another example of what O2O companies can do with data. "Through our Baidu Take Out service we are delivering food in less than one hour. If you want to deliver even faster and you have multi-point deliveries this is where the technology comes in handy," says Kaiser. "That is where the map and how you optimize your route makes the real difference in a service. You have to think that the delivery guy is normally one guy on one electric bike with a battery charge that needs to last one day. He has an 80-kilometer range and can make 20 trips a day. Thanks to data we aim to go up to 30 trips a day. It is a totally different game played with logistics and technology," says Kaiser. "Data and algorithms are the tools that are helping us move beyond and keep on improving our services and performance," says Sharon.

This clearly shows that in China the online world will increasingly control the intelligence needed for the offline world and smart devices will be fully integrated into daily life, thus becoming essential tools to do even the simplest tasks like delivering three-dollar noodles and beer.

It Is All About Social

Shelby 2012-2-18

As the dark gray Bentley Flying Spur crosses the Lok Ma Chou customs border from Hong Kong to China, Jeffrey Kang gazes out of his window from the back seat. He is thinking about his first time in Shenzhen many years before. That first trip to the city that made him so successful was not quite as comfortable as this one.

During the half hour drive from the border to his office in Shenzhen Nanshan district, Jeffrey chats with his son on WeChat.

Since he needs to spend half of the week in Shenzhen, he wants to make sure that he remains close to his son who lives in Hong Kong. When Jeffrey was a student, communicating with family while he was away from home was not as convenient. Technology has changed people's lives dramatically and Jeffrey likes to think that he has played a part in this.

Jeffrey, whose Chinese name is Kang Jingwei, has done pretty well for himself and his family, but life has not always been easy. He comes from a working class family from Chongqing, in Sichuan Province, deep in the heart of China. He grew up in the 1980s when China was an underdeveloped country.

Despite their modest lifestyle, Jeffrey's parents taught him to be ambitious. His parents were believers in the American dream: the freedom to pursue a great job, to own a house and to attain upward social mobility. They taught him that through hard work, success could be achieved. His father recommended that Jeffrey travel to the West to learn about a new culture. This was one of the most important pieces of advice he was given.

When choosing his university in 1987, Jeffrey was encouraged by his father to study in a place where he could expand his mind and seek new opportunities. Jeffrey picked Guangzhou, 1,500 kilometers away from home. Not far from Hong Kong, Guangzhou was opened to overseas investments in 1984. Foreign companies were allowed to establish factories and liaison offices. To Jeffrey and his family, the coast with its foreign influence represented the future.

In the late 1980s, Guangzhou was a colorless city, with Soviet-style buildings, few cars and polluting factories located in the middle of residential areas. It was quite a contrast to the current Guangzhou, which is now home to some of the tallest skyscrapers in the world.

At university, Jeffrey majored in electronic engineering, following in the footsteps of some of the most famous presidents of China, including Jiang Zeming and Hu Jintao. Jeffrey and his generation believed that China could only progress with advances in science and technology. It was their slogan and dream.

Every summer Jeffrey would travel home by train. At the time, most trains were still powered by steam so journeys could last several days. The trips felt like marathons. If travelers had enough money, they could buy a soft seat or soft bed ticket. Most of the passengers, however, would travel in a class called "hard seats," wooden benches shared by three passengers per side. The carriages were reasonably clean at the start of the journey but usually filthy by the time the train reached its destination.

It often took Jeffrey two days to reach home. Sometimes, though he had purchased tickets for a seat, Jeffrey would have to stand, or lie down on the floor below the wooden benches because the train was so full. He was 17. No matter how grueling the rides were, he and his classmates were happy. It was their first time leaving their hometowns to study in a different place. They were exploring a new world and they felt free.

During that time, trains had none of the modern conveniences of today. There were no flat screen TVs, smartphones, or iPads. The luckiest people would have a Panasonic radio or Sony Walkman to keep them company during the journey. Train cars would turn into communities with people enjoying music and sharing stories. Those radios made a lasting impression in Jeffrey's mind.

After graduation, Jeffrey decided to try his luck in Shenzhen, one of the most advanced cities in southeast China on the border of Hong Kong.

Once a green valley surrounded by mountains where farmers grew vegetables, Shenzhen was turned into a Special Economic Zone in the 1980s. The Chinese government had decided to reform the national economy by creating ad hoc economic and technological areas of which Shenzhen was the most famous.

Jeffrey was eager to move to Shenzhen and put his degree to work. However, access to the city required a special permit that he did not possess. Undaunted, he boarded the train from Guangzhou to Shenzhen and made it safely through the border. After knocking on the door of every major company in Shenzhen, he eventually found a low-level job in an audio and radio components factory.

Life on the assembly line was not easy; he was part of an endless line of workers connecting microscopic components. Despite the drudgery, Jeffrey remembered the lessons his parents had taught him and continued to believe that hard work would allow him to attain a better life someday.

At 21, Jeffrey reached a turning point in his life, when the Panasonic Corporation, the very company that produced the radio he had listened to on those long train rides home, offered him a job. It was the early 1990s and Panasonic was actively recruiting sales engineers with technological backgrounds. With his electronics degree and boundless energy, Jeffrey was a perfect candidate. His first Japanese boss liked him right away.

During his years at Panasonic, Huawei, the famous Chinese telecom company known for manufacturing routers, high-speed networks and mobile phones, became his first client. This was the beginning of an extensive and precious network of contacts that Jeffrey would develop.

Good timing has been a constant for Jeffrey. After the Tiananmen Square protests in 1989, China had once again shut itself off from the world. It was not until 1992, when Deng Xiaoping revisited Shenzhen and requested that China resume trade, that Shenzhen really took off.

In 1995, Jeffrey again found himself in the right place at the right time. After four years of working for Panasonic, he had accumulated enough experience to start his own electronic components trading business. Panasonic became one of his first customers.

In 2000, riding the dotcom boom that had spread to China, Jeffrey founded his first Internet company, raising money from important institutions such as SoftBank and Acer Venture. He launched the first online video company similar to YouTube and WebEx. Unfortunately, the world was not yet ready for streaming, and after three years the business failed.

Fortunately for Jeffrey, his trading business was booming and in January 2005 it became the first company from Shenzhen to list on the NASDAQ. It was called COGO, later renamed Viewtran, and grew to a market capitalization of 800 million USD in just three years.

Early in 2010, Jeffrey sensed a change in his industry. Impressed by the impact that e-commerce and social media were having on traditional industries, he felt that it was time to bring his business online.

Procurement of electronic components in China was complicated. Hundreds of suppliers were incapable of marketing themselves to millions of potential customers around the world, while small buyers with limited bargaining power struggled to find suitable suppliers.

Jeffrey realized that an online platform could make component procurement much more efficient. Instead of simply creating a directory like Alibaba.com, he envisioned an e-commerce site that could also provide offline after-sales services. He would combine his offline trading business with a new online business model. His new company Cogobuy was born.

However, an online-to-offline (O2O) e-commerce site was not enough. Jeffrey and his team wanted to revolutionize the semiconductor business. It was time to go social.

Cogobuy partnered with Tencent to develop a WeChat application. Jeffrey and his team realized that they could bring the advantages of a social network into the semiconductor industry. Suppliers and clients were now talking to each other.

In September 2013, riding the wave of the emerging trend called C2B (consumer to business) that is changing Chinese manufacturing industry and allowing consumers and producers to interact in a new way, Cogobuy launched Ingdan.com, known in English as Hardeggs, a WeChat community promoting idea and knowledge exchange between electronics designers and engineers in China. It is a revolutionary tool that connects manufacturers and hardware inventors.

In July 2014, Cogobuy was listed on the Hong Kong Stock Exchange raising 177 million USD with a valuation of almost 800 million USD. At 44 years old, Jeffrey had already listed two businesses in two different continents. His positive thinking was continuing to pay off.

Social Is Embedded in the Business Model

Jeffrey and his Cogobuy model show that social and commerce, when combined, can bring successful results even in the least likely of industries.

In 2007 and 2008 Jeffrey and his team looked at social networks, in particular Facebook, as a business tool. As Facebook use is banned in China, they were wondering what could become the Chinese version of Facebook. Ren Ren, the famous Chinese social network, seemed a likely candidate, but further research showed that it was only popular among students.

"When Tencent WeChat arrived, we suddenly realized that it could be Facebook's mobile version," said Jeffrey during one of our interviews. We were at his art gallery in the center of a new development zone in Shenzhen called The Loft. Jeffrey and his wife decided to start a gallery to help emerging Chinese painters. They understand how difficult it is to break through and want to give back to the community.

Jeffrey was playing with his brand new Airwheel X3, a hands-free Segway-alike, and was trying to teach me how to use it, but it looked tricky. He loves technological gadgets and he is always on the lookout for new things. This spirit of adventure carried over to his business with social networks.

"In 2011 we already understood the power of an application like WeChat. How powerful social media can be and how it could also be used for business. That is when we decided to partner with WeChat," Jeffrey explained.

In 2011, Cogobuy worked hard to understand how to turn an industry run by blue chip corporations and engineers into a warmer environment. Rather than regarding their engineers as just employees, Cogobuy saw them as a community exchanging ideas. Even a cold sector like business-to-business could be social.

"We realized that eventually decisions are made by people. If we were able to develop a community and connect everybody using a mobile social application like LinkedIn, we would be able to exchange ideas and conduct marketing with the very people that have the decision power to purchase inside a company," Jeffrey told me.

"Through our WeChat community we can inform engineers about new industry developments, such as how a new hardware component can speed up mobile payment processing in the smartphone they are developing," Jeffrey said. "By doing this, we create a business demand that we can service through our e-commerce platform. Engineers can also give feedback as to what components suppliers should develop in the near future."

"The reason we have not seen any successful B2B e-commerce companies in the last ten years is because everyone is focusing on B2B as a pure transaction business. We changed the idea by adding the social element. This has sparked a revolution in our industry and will definitely cross over to other industries," said Jeffrey.

As Jeffrey pointed out, the combination of social and commerce is not only revolutionary in traditional industries like manufacturing. It is also becoming embedded in the new business models of offline industries that are migrating online. JP Gan, the Managing Director of Qiming Venture Partners, one of China's most famous venture capital funds gave me some examples of these new models and how they work.

"What we are seeing now is just the beginning," said JP during our interview. His office walls are lined with framed photos of successful companies they have invested in from Internet to healthcare to cleantech. JP firmly believes in the success of combining social and commerce across many other industries.

"There will be more industries going online, such as, for example, manufacturing, healthcare and finance, using a combination of O2O strategies and social media. There is absolutely no doubt of that. Robin Li of Baidu said that "There will not be an Internet company in the future," every company has to be an Internet company to survive," predicted JP.

"In addition to retail, we are seeing many other sectors empowered by the Internet, such as healthcare," said JP. Qiming has co-invested with Tencent in a company connecting hospitals, doctors and patients. "The company creates electronic medical records for patients and helps patients to make appointments with doctors. One of the advantages of bringing the business online is that you can add a social network element so that patients can talk to each other. Doctors are spending more time online both learning medical information but also talking to patients."

"We actually go into the hospitals to help them to manage their systems and patients. We are taking online the offline world of hospitals. This is making the whole system more efficient. You can make healthcare cheaper and better," added JP.

As entire sectors such as automotive, healthcare and finance are moving online in China, O2O and social will prove formidable weapons to create efficiencies.

"We have seen a lot of industrial sectors that have layer after layer of wholesalers and middleman; each one is fighting for small margins," JP explained.

"There are hundreds of companies that profit on relationships and asymmetry of information. Their value added is being information consolidators. However, each middleman adds a cost to the final cost of the product. We see a number of sectors that can be streamlined just like Cogobuy is doing in the semiconductor industry. Eventually the cost saving will pass to the consumers," said JP.

JP feels that WeChat is an excellent example of an application that combines social and commerce. "WeChat is a very advanced application and I prefer it to WhatsApp. WeChat is also a better social network than Facebook. When I open Facebook it takes me 30 seconds to figure out what is going on, it has too many features. WeChat is immediate, pictures and chat."

As JP told me, this is only the beginning of how the Internet and social networks are changing traditional industries.

Social commerce in China is not just about posting videos and pictures. Chinese turn to social media to solve real life problems, to seek advice from friends and opinion leaders, and to decide what products to buy or not to buy.

The Traffic Economy and the Fan Economy

To understand the difference in usage between Eastern and Western social networks and how they convert traffic into sales, I went to Hong Kong to meet with a seasoned expert in media and advertising, Viveca Chan.

Viveca has been in the advertising business for over 30 years and is the Chairman and CEO of the WE Marketing Group. She has won numerous awards including the Top 100 Entrepreneurs in China and the 100 Most Influential Women in Advertising by Ad Age. She has extensive experience in advising Chinese and foreign brands on branding and marketing.

"Social and commerce in China have two peculiarities," explained Viveca. "The first is that unlike people in the West, Chinese consumers use social networks extensively to interact with brands."

"By nature, Chinese like to post things, comment and share. They like to share a lot. In the West, users are active through Instagram, Facebook and Twitter etc. Social networks are seen as a very intimate way to communicate. You share your things with your friends. But in China it is different. If you look, for example, at a tool like Weibo, the Chinese Twitter-like microblogging service, you can actually find that a lot of branding activities are carried on through it. Chinese want to know what the brands are doing, whether they are creating new products etc.," said Viveca.

The second peculiarity is that Chinese purchasing behavior is very social. "Chinese like to share and tell people what they have bought, while in the West people do not necessarily share their experience," Viveca explained.

The growing number of acquisitions that are taking place in the Chinese market is a clear indicator that none of the BAT-X companies wants to lose the social commerce game. In particular the two titans, Alibaba and Tencent, are fighting head to head.

Alibaba has purchased a stake in Weibo, thus linking its e-commerce platforms Taobao and Tmall to a microblog. Meanwhile the mobile and social company Tencent has purchased a stake in online retailer JD.com, thus connecting mobile and social to e-commerce.

If Alibaba and Tencent are both combining social with commerce will a unique model eventually evolve? Most importantly, will this model be social commerce?

On a Monday afternoon in October, I took a high-speed elevator to the 60th floor of the IFC tower in Hong Kong to meet with venture capitalist John Lindfors who runs the Asian operations of the global investment group Digital Sky Technologies, or DST Global.

Founded by entrepreneur Yuri Milner, who has famously invested in major Internet companies such as Facebook, Zynga, Groupon, Twitter and Airbnb, DST Global has several major investment holdings in Asia.

I asked John, with his expertise in both in Western and Asian tech companies, what he envisions for the future.

"Social commerce is not going to replace the way people do commerce but a significant part of China e-commerce is going to have social features," he said. "There is a huge social element which is about to be added to e-commerce."

Viveca had a similar opinion. "I believe that eventually we will have two purchasing models. When you look at an e-commerce website like Tmall, what it does is drive traffic and convert it into sales. On the other side of the spectrum you have an application like WeChat, which is not about traffic; it is about fans. Therefore, we can say that we have two different economies: the traffic economy and the fan economy. In the future there will be a shift from a pure traffic economy to a traffic and fan economy; they will coexist."

According to Viveca and other experts, however, the fan economy is still in its infancy. "Right now most of the business is still carried on Alibaba's platforms. We are still living in a traffic economy. Alibaba is primarily an e-commerce platform and it is driving e-commerce very well by generating a huge volume of traffic."

"Tencent has started to carry on e-commerce on WeChat and uses a very different strategy from Alibaba. While Tmall and Taobao are open to everybody, WeChat is a closed system, where you can only talk and interact with your friends. You can invite them to shop on your shop but always through a closed network," she said.

Viveca explained that the difference between opening a store on an e-commerce platform like Alibaba and on a social platform like WeChat is like opening a shop in a big shopping mall, borrowing other people's traffic, versus opening a shop in a small alley with limited traffic, but where your friends will come and buy because they know you. "As long as you have a lot of friends, your little shop can still do a good business," said Viveca.

Viveca thinks that another reason the fan economy has not kicked in yet is because WeChat is so protective of its brand. "Tencent does not want to become commercialized and does not want WeChat to lose its essence. At the moment it is the best way to reach your friends without interruptions, such as pop up ads. Tmall is different, you go there to buy and want the interruptions to learn about the best promotions. You go there to be entertained. So the two models each represent a different kind of purchasing experience," she explained.

One example of a successful fan economy platform that has integrated e-commerce with social is Mogujie, a popular fashion application, which has been valued over 1 billion USD in its Series C round financing in June 2014.[1] Mogujie originally started as a picture viewing website, just like Pinterest. Users would upload selfies taken with the merchandise they just bought and then comment on each other's purchases.

Mogujie users are generally "real" young people—college students, secretaries, etc. and not professional models—which makes the site seems more authentic. Users give feedback on how other users combine clothes and accessories and then make suggestions. Mogujie is a form of online window shopping. This is where the social element comes in.

Qiming Ventures is one of Mogujie's biggest investors and JP brought me up to speed with what is happening with the company. "The company has grown from a user base of 0 to 1 million in six months and from 1 million to 5 million within a year and a half. It has grown very fast," said JP. Mogujie has now over 100 million users, and counting.[2]

JP confirmed what Viveca had told me. "The idea behind Mogujie is a natural evolution of purchasing habits. People buy and then they share. Also, merchants are socializing with their customers when selling their products."

Mogujie started as a social network for fashion, but it soon transformed into a full-fledged e-commerce platform when it realized that a fan economy could be as powerful as a traffic economy.

"At the beginning Mogujie was generating a lot of sales leads to Taobao, which would pay Mogujie commissions in return," JP explained. When consumers look at pictures and click, they are redirected to Taobao shops. "But as Mogujie volume increased, Taobao became worried about its explosive growth and decided to adopt a different commission system causing Mogujie to lose 30 percent of its revenues overnight. I guessed Mogujie became just too big," said JP.

"We and Mogujie both went back to the drawing board to work on a new revenue model," he told me. "The management team got very smart and thought that, since we cannot make any more revenues from Taobao, why don't we make our own e-commerce instead?"

After Chinese New Year 2014, Mogujie started to acquire merchants, now over 10,000,[3] and launched its own marketplace. "Mogujie has evolved into a marketplace for female apparel. We try to offer a better experience by adding a social element. The smart merchants not only post pictures of their merchandise but also show merchandise from other sources like Korea and Japan acting as an aggregator," said JP.

"Mogujie is the quintessential fan economy. When I download Mogujie and use it I basically stay in a closed environment just like WeChat. I look at the picture and I am connected directly to the merchant and then the merchant delivers to me. I never leave the app. There I can find everything," he explained.

"When you buy on Taobao you have a huge selection but sometimes you cannot trust what you are getting. When you are on Mogujie it is like applying a kind of a filter. You see the girl and what she is wearing and since she is a real customer, you trust what you buy a bit more."

I learned from Viveca and John that the fan economy is a different shopping experience than the traffic economy, and as JP noted, "One does not exclude the other."

*   *   *

It is 11:30 a.m. and Violette is reviewing the merchandising reports she received last night. Her phone suddenly rings; her friend Tracy is waiting for her at the restaurant downstairs. Violette did not realize it was already lunchtime.

She descends to the lobby and walks out into the October wind, barely able to hold onto her black Borsalino hat. She turns right, walks through the alley and quickly reaches the restaurant.

Tracy is waiting on the second floor, she has already found a table and ordered their favorites: stir-fried broccoli and sour and spicy soups. Tracy looks very excited and says that she has something to share. With her black top, gray jeans and English lace-up Oxfords, Tracy looks very elegant.

Tracy is a fashion blogger and also works for a fashion e-commerce website. She often gives styling and wardrobe advice to Violette. She recently wrote an article on a Dior blazer that was read by 100,000 readers. Tracy unlocks her iPhone and opens her WeChat page. She has just finished the layout for her own WeChat store and is now showing it to Violette for feedback.

Tracy has many friends in the fashion industry who have purchased clothes and accessories at hefty discounts but never used them. She set up her WeChat store to sell these items collected from her circle of friends and has already had many requests.

Violette asks why she has opted to set up her store on WeChat rather than Taobao. Tracy tells her that the admission procedure for a Taobao shop has become very lengthy, whereas on WeChat, it is now possible for a merchant to open a store in just a few hours.

Tracy wants to start small and market to her circle of friends. She uses WeChat Moments, the Facebook-like function of the social application, to share her blog articles and educate her friends. It is all connected in the same application. A mobile social network allows her to communicate with customers, gather feedback and make recommendations.

Violette is impressed. She gives Tracy some feedback based on what she learned from her recent meetings with the marketing agency and suggests a couple of layout changes. She also placed an order; she couldn't resist the Salvatore Ferragamo black silk scarf with the purple butterflies.

Everything for Everyone

Before interviewing John, I watched one of his videos on YouTube where he introduced China e-commerce features to a crowd of startuppers in Helsinki. It was November 2012.

When I met him my first question was: "What has changed in China e-commerce since your speech in Helsinki?" He told me that user numbers had grown exponentially and that the market had evolved quite substantially.

"At the beginning, people only shopped on Taobao. Then, two years ago Tmall started to generate traffic. This time it was a high-end platform that was catching up with a mid-to-low-level platform. Then JD.com with its focus on consumer electronics gained an important market share and, finally, VIP.com emerged as a leader in flash sales. In just two years Chinese e-commerce has seen the explosive growth of big independent e-commerce players," John explained.

"The growth of these companies' market share indicates that consumers have become more sophisticated. Rather than going to Taobao and spending half an hour to find an item, people now go straight to the site they know and trust for those specific products. This search mentality did not exist two years ago. The one-solution-fits-all mentality is still widespread because 70 percent of the market is still Taobao dominated, but an increasing percentage of consumers are going directly to specialized websites," John told me.

The majority of Internet users in 2007 were retired people playing games online. It seems almost impossible that in just few years the user segmentation and sophistication level has increased so much. Even more staggering is seeing some small e-commerce companies becoming multi-billion dollar empires in such a short time.

According to Jack Ma, the user sophistication level is just at its infancy. At the SoftBank Word Conference 2014 held in July, right before Alibaba's initial public offering, Jack Ma talked about the new trend hitting the e-commerce world: C2B or consumer to business.

With C2B, the customers essentially dictate what manufacturers produce. Mobile phones and social commerce allow manufacturers to collect and leverage a mountain of consumer data that is used to streamline product assortment.

A study by Alibaba provides one example of the kind of information C2B can provide to manufacturers. As reported by Lily Kuo in Quartz in November 2014: "Earlier this summer a group of data crunchers looking at underwear sales at Alibaba came across a curious trend: women who bought larger bra sizes also tended to spend more . . . This data nugget is an example of the kinds of detail the company gleans from the millions of orders placed daily on its e-commerce platforms."[4]

The ability to gather data is a game changer for manufacturers, and customization is the first example. As reported by Tech in Asia in July 2014, Jack Ma, speaking at the SoftBank World event, mentioned that: ". . . instead of companies producing thousands of t-shirts of the same color, customers will soon completely dictate to companies what they need and only companies that accommodate them will thrive. Not 10,000 red t-shirts, but 10,000 t-shirts of 10,000 colors."[5]

But how does customization and C2B actually work? Fan Fan, the Taobao and Tmall fashion entrepreneur connecting customers with the backbone of China manufacturing, gave me a good example.

On her WeChat Moment page, she publishes her new campaigns and uses them to test ideas and gather feedback from her customers and friends.

When customers feel that something is missing from the collection, they can suggest a new item. With her direct relationship with the factories, Fan Fan has the ability to roll out samples and have a new online collection ready in as little as one week. Not even Zara can do that.

With this sort of data, companies are able to understand, by consumer segment, what customers really want and can react quickly to meet their needs. This means that soon everything will be available for everyone.

C2B is not limited to selling shoes and bags. In a larger sense, C2B also means that the customers themselves are becoming part of the invention process for all sorts of products and services.

From Everybody to Everything

At the moment, big data technology is at its infancy. As Joseph Tsai, Alibaba's Executive Vice Chairman, declared to Quartz.[6] He believes that this is just the tip of the iceberg. Data has tremendous potential and by leveraging it Alibaba can make its operations more efficient and consumers more satisfied.

Once not only people but also objects are connected, they will generate an endless stream of data that businesses will use to streamline processes and offer better goods and services to their customers.

As Bruce, Kaado's inventor, told me in Beijing, soon we'll have refrigerators capable of figuring out what we need and then automatically placing an order. It is called the Internet of Things, or IoT.

China is placing a big bet on IoT and smartphone maker Xiaomi is already moving in that direction. Qiming Ventures is one of Xiaomi's earliest investors and JP confirmed that "Xiaomi has a number of investments in the Internet of Things with the idea of using its smartphone to control everything around you. It will be the center of home electronics."

As China is moving from everybody online to everything online, Jeffrey believes that it might soon be the leader in the IoT business because "China is a hot bed for hardware and most of the IoT components are already manufactured here."

However, if China wants to lead in IoT, it needs to move upstream; it cannot be merely a manufacturer, it must foster innovation from the ground up.

Jeffrey and his company Cogobuy have just found a way to do exactly this, i.e. moving the well-known Shenzhen hardware-manufacturing cluster upstream.

When entrepreneurs and inventors need to find an effective way to go from an idea to a commercial product, Kickstarter, the well-known U.S. online crowdfunding platform, has proven to be a valuable ally.

Since 2009, Kickstarter has revolutionized the invention process. Inventors pitch their ideas to the public and if perspective customers validate them, they can finance the inventions by joining a crowd-funding campaign.

Though quite helpful, Kickstarter has not solved one of the inventors' most complicated issues. Once financing is in place, inventors still need to find suppliers to manufacture their prototypes and then find a network to distribute their product. Failing that, their ideas remain confined to a clever marketing campaign.

Cogobuy's Ingdan.com platform was invented to address this exact challenge. The platform understands that innovation can come from the ground up. As entrepreneurs and innovators build more and more customized products, they need someone to help them with small productions that could potentially be scaled.

Developing a prototype and scaling are among the biggest challenges for inventors. First, it is difficult to source the right manufacturer. Then, budgeting for the prototype can be like answering a riddle. Finally, finding a distributor for small quantities can be challenging.

When Cogobuy was developing Ingdan.com, it intended to solve these exact problems. Not only does the innovative platform connect a community of inventors with hardware manufacturers in China, but it also assists hardware inventors with everything from prototyping to distribution.

Finally, Ingdan.com allows inventors to place their products online on the e-commerce platform JD.com. This means that the entire loop is closed and the platform can assist with a 360-degree approach.

Cogobuy and Ingdan.com demonstrate how connecting customers to suppliers has made invention in China accessible to virtually everyone and what China's IoT revolution might soon look like.

Moving East (and West)

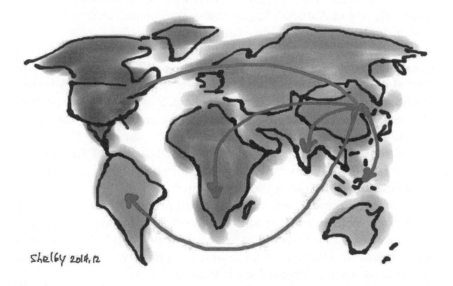

Shelby 2014.12

Before boarding my flight to Jakarta to interview the father of Indonesia's version of Taobao, I stopped at a book kiosk and skimmed through the titles. A blue cover with the title *Zero to One* caught my attention. It was the latest book by Peter Thiel, the famous PayPal co-founder and one of Silicon Valley's most successful thinkers and venture capitalists.

I purchased the book, put it in my bag and boarded the aircraft. I read it in one sitting and was intrigued by its provocative and counterintuitive teachings.

In particular, I found myself reflecting on two questions contained in the book: "What important truth do very few people agree with you on?" and "What valuable company is nobody building?"

The first is Peter Thiel's question when interviewing someone for a job. The second is its business version. I mulled those concepts in my mind for a while unaware that in a few hours I would hear two very special answers.

The following day I arrived at Startup Asia Jakarta, a technology event where I met William Tanuwijaya. A young visionary entrepreneur, he had successfully created an e-commerce platform inspired by Alibaba's Taobao. He had just received substantial investments from SoftBank, one of Alibaba's key investors, and Sequoia Capital, one of Silicon Valley's highest caliber venture capital firms.

William was in the media room, behind the main stage, answering questions from journalists and young fans. When he finished, we moved over to a corner to begin our interview. As he put his brown leather bag on the chair, I noticed a copy of *Zero to One* in the pocket. He was reading it too. The book soon became an important reference throughout our talk.

Born in 1981 in a small town of Sumatra, one of Indonesia's biggest islands, William came from a small plantation town that had neither a university nor a shopping center.

William's grandfather, once an entrepreneur, had passed the business to William's father and uncles who, unfortunately, had not been as successful. The business went bankrupt when William was still a child, and his father took a job in a local factory. William was not raised in an entrepreneurial environment.

After graduating from high school, William's father and uncle sent him to Jakarta, situated on the island of Java, to get a university degree. They wanted him to be more successful than the prior generations of the family and to see the world.

At age 18, he enrolled in computer science at the Bina Nusantara University. During the day he studied and attended classes. At night he worked at an Internet café to support his family and pay for his father's medical bills.

William worked as the Internet café operator until graduation and received free online access. In 1999 Internet rates in Indonesia were very expensive, and one of his job's perks was to see the world, though, for the moment, only online.

His work shifts were long, from 10 p.m. until 9 a.m. every day. During those quiet hours, which he called "the zombie hours," he had plenty of time to play games, read and surf the Internet. He taught himself to program HTML/CSS and rarely went to classes. He loves to say that he graduated from an Internet café and not from a university.

Growing up in a small town, his hobby was reading. He would devour his books but had to wait months for new ones to arrive. The Internet gave him immediate and limitless access to information. He realized that the Internet was going to change the world.

After graduating in 2003, he looked for an Internet job. Unfortunately, large Internet companies like Facebook and Google did not have representative offices in Indonesia at that point. He found work at several software companies including a games publisher, an airline reservation system, and in 2007 he joined a company active in SMS broadcasting services. To supplement his income William also worked at night as a freelance web designer.

The SMS company provided subscription services such as informing soccer fans through SMS when their favorite team had scored a goal. William knew that soon people would stop paying for SMS content and instead access information through the Internet. As Peter Thiel posed in his book, it was time to think about what valuable business nobody was building.

Two observations helped William find an answer. First, there was not yet a trusted environment for online transactions. Second, more and more people were interested in selling online but weren't sure how to go about it.

Since his Internet café years, William had been spending more time online than offline. Eventually, he managed to become an online forum super moderator acting as a third party supervisor. As eBay did not yet exist in Indonesia, people were using this forum not only to chat but also to sell products, similar to Craigslist in the U.S.

William noticed that buying and selling on the forum was becoming more difficult. People wanted to meet face to face to exchange goods and money. Since Indonesia is an archipelago country with more than 17,000 islands, people on the forum often lived in different cities or islands. To complete a transaction, buyers had to first wire the funds and only then would merchants send their products. At the early stage this method worked well, but as online purchasing gained popularity, scams started to appear, and trust became an issue.

As a supervisor, William was often asked to help when someone had fallen victim of a scam. However, he had no power to enforce any corrective measures. He couldn't help customers with refunds or prevent a scam from recurring; all he had was an email and IP address. This is when he realized that if online commerce was going to succeed, it needed a different kind of platform, one that would generate trust.

William also realized that more and more Indonesian family-owned shops wanted to sell online. Through his freelance work, he often met with mom and pop businesses, which wanted to create websites. Each of them wanted to set up an Amazon-like e-commerce website to sell their products throughout Indonesia. However, family businesses had very little capital to invest and limited knowledge about setting up a website and generating traffic.

William saw that on one side there were merchants willing to sell, and on the other buyers willing to buy online. However, there was not a proper method to connect them yet.

These were the observations that made him realize that the business no one was building was a platform where people could buy and sell online in a trusted environment.

He went back to the Internet to research which model would successfully apply to Indonesia. He studied Amazon and eBay as well as the Japanese Rakuten and the Korean G-Market. Finally, he turned to China and saw that Alibaba had created its own eBay-like market-place called Taobao. This was the model William had been looking for. It solved the very same issues that Indonesia e-commerce would have to address. With its thousands of islands, recreating an Amazon-like direct sales model in Indonesia would require building ware-houses in all the first tier cities, which was simply unthinkable. Taobao, however, was not built like an e-commerce company but rather as a platform connecting vendors and buyers.

William approached his boss and told him bluntly that the SMS business had no future and that they should build an Internet platform. At first his boss did not understand what William meant. To keep things simple, he told his boss that they should build the "eBay of Indonesia," since he knew he wouldn't understand the Taobao reference with his limited knowledge of e-commerce plat-forms. William knew that they could build the valuable business that no one had built as Thiel teaches in his book. Thiel believes that every company should pick a niche where it is likely to become a monopoly and then grow bigger and bigger as Google and Facebook did.

Though his boss did not really understand William, he was kind enough to introduce him to a group of local wealthy investors. Between 2007 and 2009 he would pitch to several entrepreneurs unsuccessfully. Eventually all of them would ask the same five questions. Two were business related and three personal. From a business point of view, investors did not see an exit strategy. There was not yet a success story to tell. They would ask William whether he knew of any Indonesian entrepreneurs who had become rich with the Internet: "Who is the Bill Gates of Indonesia?" There wasn't one. "This is not Silicon Valley. There is no local success story to justify our investment in your business," they would tell him.

The second question was related to how William would fight off the competition. If the need for this business existed, big brands like eBay and Rakuten would inevitably arrive and crush him. "International competitors have bottomless pockets and it would be very hard, if not impossible, for you to beat them," they would say. These business questions were relatively easy for William to digest, but those related to his credibility were more difficult. Investors would ask about William's family background. In Indonesia, carrying a good family name was essential. William's background was too modest for their taste. Next, the potential investors would inquire about his studies. Unfortunately, William had not attended a prestigious university. Finally, they would ask about his previous entrepreneurial successes, but he had none to offer them. At the end of the pitch, the investors would caution him not to dream too big.

William did not give up and conducted more research on the names behind the most successful Internet entrepreneurs. He would study their backgrounds and found that most of them had never studied business. Some did not even have a degree. He then realized that the only thing he really lacked was a success story, and unless he built one for himself, no one else would. This was a turning point in his life.

In 2009, his boss realized that William's predictions were correct and decided to provide the initial funding for the platform. William cautioned that e-commerce was a long-term business, and that it could not be monetized from day one. Nevertheless, his boss was determined and offered to invest up to 250,000 USD to start. His boss proposed that his nephew, Leontinus Alpha Edison, become William's partner, and the company shares be allocated as follows: the boss would hold 80 percent and William and Leon would each hold 10 percent. William did not think twice; this was his ticket. He knew that 10 percent of something was better than 100 percent of nothing. He also knew that Jakarta was not Silicon Valley and that, as Charles Schwab once said, "The best way to succeed is where you are with what you have."

After the company was established, William and his partner attended a university fair to recruit employees. They rented the two biggest booths in the fair hoping to get a lot of applications. They received none. Indonesian graduates were all seeking corporate jobs. So they started with what they had and after six months, on Indonesia's Independence Day in 2009, they launched their business.

Around that time, the JW Marriott and Ritz-Carlton Hotels in Jakarta were hit by separate bombings five minutes apart. The twin suicide bombings came four years after the last serious terrorist attack in Bali. Tokopedia and the merchants wanted to let everybody know how outraged they were, and decided to support a netizen movement called Indonesia Unite by selling t-shirts on their website with the slogan: "We are not afraid." This is how Indonesians were first introduced to Tokopedia.

In March 2010, competitors began to appear on the horizon, just as investors had predicted. eBay partnered with Indonesia's largest telecommunication company, Rakuten with the media conglomerate MNC (Media Nusantara Citra), and finally Naspers with Multiply, a social media platform from the U.S.

On paper it was impossible to beat them, but the beauty of the Internet is that anyone can challenge the status quo, even the underdogs. Three things helped Tokopedia win the battle. First, while its competitors were spending millions of dollars educating consumers on e-commerce, Tokopedia was lean and cost conscious, spending a mere 300 USD for its monthly advertising budget while capitalizing on the efforts of its competitors. Second, Tokopedia's small size allowed it to make decisions more quickly than its competitors, a key advantage in the Internet business. Finally, it fought with a do-or-die attitude, while multinationals could write off their investment if not successful. After three years Tokopedia killed its competition.

In October 2014, Tokopedia surprised everyone when it set the record for the largest round of funding in Indonesian startup history.

SoftBank and Sequoia Capital agreed to invest 100 million USD. William had always felt emotionally connected to SoftBank, the Japanese telecommunication and Internet company, since it was founded in the same year he was born. William was also inspired by SoftBank's founder, Masayoshi Son, whose vision to build a company that would outlast him aligned with William's dream of building a company that would last for decades. Along with SoftBank came Sequoia, an early investor in big tech companies like Apple and Google. The fund had seen the roller-coaster phases of big tech entrepreneurs. It was like a time machine for William, as Sequoia would know how to help him in the years to come.

Looking at *Zero to One* sticking out of the pocket of William's bag, I decided to ask him, "What important truth do very few people agree with you on?" His answer would definitely grant him a job. The important truth for him is that he has allowed Indonesia to celebrate its first successful tech story. However, not everyone agrees with him. People say that he is a sell-out since he sold equity to foreigners. He does not know why this kind of mentality still exists, but he thinks it is both hypocritical and dangerous. For example, Jakarta has the highest tweet volume of any city in the world.[1] William told me that Indonesians laugh at their local social media. He believes that choosing based on nationalism is the wrong mindset. Smart people choose products that work, regardless of where they are from. William believes that, had he not chosen to open his company with capable partners, Indonesia might not have been on the tech map for years.

Spreading into Asia

William and Tokopedia are part of one of Asia's most promising e-commerce markets. Investors are setting their sights on Indonesia's tech sector and on its economy. After a period of eclipse during the Asian financial crisis in the late 1990s, Indonesia's GDP has been growing robustly since 2010.

During my trip to Jakarta I noticed a strong will among the people to develop their country, though a lot of work still needs to be done. Optimism is in the air, the energy is palpable and streets are busier than ever. Indonesians abroad are traveling back to their homeland to catch this big opportunity. The population is young, energetic and excited about the future.

The Internet and the mobile market are playing fundamental roles in this growth. "Soon 100 million people, out of 250 million, will be connected," said Agus Nurudin, Managing Director of Nielsen Indonesia, at the Euromoney's Indonesia Investment Forum 2014. Fifteen million smart devices were sold in 2014 and according to the Consensus forecast in the three-year period between 2012 and 2015, around 75 million smartphones will have been sold in Indonesia. "Growth is exponential and accelerating," said Agus.

Indonesia's mass adoption of mobile phones and smart devices has much in common with that of China; it is leapfrogging computers. According to Rudy Ramawy, former Country Manager for Google and now a successful venture capital investor, also speaking at the Euromoney Forum: "Indonesia is split into two countries; half is very connected and looks like Brazil's urban population, while the other half looks more like the masses of India who are features phones connected, but not really connected. This remaining 50 percent will soon come online using a mobile phone without ever purchasing a laptop," Rudy said.

The advent of cheap and powerful smart devices, like Xiaomi's handsets, is driving an online retail revolution. According to research by Frost & Sullivan, Indonesia's growing middle class and young population will push e-commerce revenues from an estimated 1 billion USD in 2013 to 10 billion USD by 2016. "There is great potential here and five years from now Indonesian e-commerce will be a very common tool for everybody to use," said William.

As I witnessed in China, e-commerce in Indonesia is not only about selling products; it is reforming a bureaucratic and inefficient system. William believes that e-commerce benefits the economy not only because it boosts consumer spending, but it also disrupts the system of middlemen. "Delivering a product across the country is expensive; there are a lot of players involved which pushes prices higher," explained William. "E-commerce is cutting out the middle-man and a lot of products will become more accessible and cheaper."

Although Indonesia is on track to become a very big Internet market, there is another country where the Chinese e-commerce model has been successful. John Lindfors, the venture capitalist heading DST Global, believes that, "The same e-commerce tsunami that has swept China will go to other parts of the world such as India." DST Global is one of the investors in India's biggest e-commerce platform, Flipkart and taxi hailing application Ola Cabs.

Though familiar with South East Asian e-commerce, I had only a rudimentary knowledge of the Indian market. I knew that India has a very important technology hub and top-quality software companies, but I was not familiar with its Internet giants. During one of my research trips to Hong Kong, I met with Heavent Malhotra, the Managing Director of Rocket Internet, India.

According to Heavent, Indian's e-commerce market has exploded since 2010, growing over 100 percent each year. Gartner believes that the market will reach 6 billion USD in consumer spending in 2015, leaping from 3.5 billion USD in 2014. "Any projection on India's growth does not show less than 70 percent year over year in the medium term," said Heavent.

After talking with Heavent, I realized that the Indian e-commerce market is in the midst of a revolution and that investors are rushing to place their bets and support the winning team. Indian e-commerce players are divided into two categories: those operating horizontally, which sell multi-industry products, and those operating vertically, which specialize in one industry like fashion, for example. "The three biggest horizontals players are Flipkart, which is the Amazon of India and now valued at billions of dollars, Amazon itself and Snapdeal, considered the Alibaba of India. Jabong is a Rocket Internet venture that specializes in fashion, and is the leader among fashion verticals," said Heavent.

Flipkart and Snapdeal demonstrate that the China e-commerce model has successfully crossed the Himalayas. Founded by former Amazon employees and based in Bangalore, India's Karnataka State, "Flipkart has seen a spectacular growth over the last few years," said Heavent. "Its earlier version was intended to be like the 'everything store,' but lately, since Alibaba gained prominence, Flipkart started to look at the Chinese marketplace with interest." Heavent believes that Flipkart will follow the emerging market's model developed by China. "In a way it is taking the best parts of the Alibaba model and of the JD.com/Amazon model," he said.

Two thousand kilometers north of Flipkart's headquarters is Uttar Pradesh State, where Snapdeal is located. Founded in Delhi in 2010 by Kunal Bahl and his partner Rohit Bansal, their e-commerce site is another important example of how Alibaba's model is becoming an

Asian franchise. Recently valued billions of USD, it counts eBay and SoftBank among its investors.

On a late Saturday afternoon in November, during a conference call from Delhi, Kunal told me his company's fascinating story. "We started as a daily deal site like Groupon, acting as a marketplace for local merchants such as restaurants, etc. During a visit to China in 2011, we noticed that product marketplaces would eventually become very big and after the trip we decided to pivot from a service marketplace into a product marketplace," Kunal explained.

Kunal and Rohit already knew that the Indian market had more in common with the Chinese market than with the market in the U.S. Both India and China had poor infrastructures, extremely value-conscious consumers and a high number of mobile users. They realized that Alibaba's Tmall and Taobao pure marketplace models would solve India's biggest issue: aggregating India's millions of small brands and sellers, which account for 95 percent of the country's retail market. Chinese marketplaces would also deliver another advantage. Using the Alibaba model, Snapdeal could afford to offer the largest assortment of products and the largest base of sellers without securing huge initial funding.

Besides selling products, Kunal and Rohit realized that Alibaba was also providing services like payment systems and loans. This inspired them to create new offerings. In 2013, Snapdeal launched its payment system called Trustpay, and in November 2014, through a partnership with banking technology platform Fino PayTech, it launched a service called "assisted e-commerce." This first of its kind partnership gives lower income individuals in semi-urban, rural and residential areas across the country access to an assortment of over 1,000 products through centers that are operated by Fino PayTech.

Kunal believes that there is still an untapped market in India. "Only 225 million Indians had Internet connectivity as of March 2014. Of these, roughly 12 percent, or 25 million, shop online. We are now catering to the remaining billion people," said Kunal. The partnership with Fino allows consumers who have no permanent address or connectivity to walk into the centers, place an order with a Fino agent, and receive their goods directly at the shop. "Suddenly, you open up a 900 million USD market," said Kunal. He believes that India's e-commerce market still has significant room for growth. "It is a dynamic time where we are experiencing an exponential growth of the market and in the next five years it will become a 100 billion USD market up from where it is now," said Kunal. Investors seem to agree with them since, after investing in Tokopedia, SoftBank poured 627 million USD into Snapdeal in November 2014 and then another 500 million USD, together with Alibaba and Foxconn, on August 2015.[2]

India and Indonesia are now on the map of the hottest tech areas in which to invest and it is becoming evident that the Chinese e-commerce model is successfully spreading outside its borders and turning into a source of inspiration for the East and the West. That is why I believe we are on the verge of a phenomenon that I have called *East-Commerce.*

The Developing Countries Model

East-Commerce is not only confined to Asia, it is moving to other emerging markets such as South America and Africa. For example, in 2014 Baidu bought a controlling stake in the Brazilian online discount company Peixe Urbano founded in Rio de Janeiro in 2010. "When we acquired the company it had 30 percent market share and now in 2015 it has 60 percent of group buying transactions. Our model definitely benefited their success," says Kaiser Kuo, Head of International Communications for Baidu. "Brazil resembles China some years ago. Maybe three to five years ago. They are both very large and emerging markets, still underpenetrated in Internet usage, yet growing very fast in penetration and predominantly mobile. Furthermore, they are both countries where there is a huge gap between the rich cosmopolitan metropolis and the far regions. This is true of Indonesia, Brazil, Nigeria, India and Thailand. Our model, in particular our O2O model, can work very well in these environments," says Kaiser.

Nigeria is definitely another example of East-Commerce. The Nigerian e-commerce website Konga.com, originally conceived with an Amazon-like model, launched its marketplace platform at the beginning of 2014 with the goal to become the Alibaba of Africa.[3] The bet has paid off as it is set to become Africa's biggest Internet company.[4]

As Kaiser confirmed to me, the e-commerce model created by China to cope with its underdeveloped retail infrastructure leverages the high penetration of smart devices, and a population with growing spending power. This model seems to be working well in emerging countries with similar needs. According to Johnson Hu, General Manager of Baidu International Business Development, speaking from the Baidu September 2015 annual conference in Beijing, the company uses the following three points to enter a target country. Baidu searches for mass populated countries whose mobile Internet is at an early development phase and with a potential to grow. Baidu then selects a specific product that can be launched in the target market. Finally, it leverages its mobile and O2O knowledge. "Whereas in the past we copied technology from abroad, now we are able to export our own products innovation and operational know-how," said Johnson.[5]

"China's online model is simply proving to be more suitable to younger economies than the developed world models," said Kunal. "While the U.S. retail infrastructure and its e-commerce model are twenty years ahead of India, the Chinese model is only about seven years ahead. China is a closer proxy to India," he added.

This leads to the conclusion that two different models seem to be emerging for two different market conditions. "We can now distinguish between developed countries and developing countries models," said Porter, the former VP for Alibaba now helping e-commerce companies build marketplaces.

Porter's conclusion is based on his on-the-ground experience with Taobao. "People know that the U.S. has developed the most mature and effective e-commerce model. It is a bit like buying a car. Everyone knows that Germany has produced some of the most advanced cars in the world," said Porter. But here is the catch: "The established model used in developed markets like the U.S., Europe and Japan does not work well in developing markets because it has been built relying on different infrastructures and market features. Therefore you need to develop a model that better suits the different market conditions of a developing economy." This is exactly what China did.

Porter believes that China e-commerce and, in particular, the Alibaba model work better for three reasons. First, it fosters entrepreneurship. "Entrepreneurship in developing countries is even bigger than in the U.S. and it is an entrepreneurship for survival, you either do or die," explained Porter. Second, marketplaces create trust. "You need to allow buyers and sellers, who do not know each other, to find a way to do commerce together," said Porter. "At

Taobao we gave vendors and buyers a live chat to replicate online the offline experience, unlike eBay and Amazon who both created a wall between buyer and seller." Third, marketplaces give access to products where retail infrastructures are still underdeveloped.

What I noticed in talking to William, Kunal, Porter and Heavent, however, is that even though China's e-commerce works well in emerging markets, there are no two emerging markets that are alike. Martin Gil, President of Coca-Cola Indonesia, speaking at the Euromoney's Indonesia Investment Forum, gave a very good example of how two emerging countries that might look similar on paper have unique features. "Coca-Cola has ten factories in Indonesia to be able to serve all the islands, compared to Vietnam which has only four." William and Kunal both agree that even though the Chinese e-commerce model works well, you cannot simply transport it to another market and begin using it. "What I want to make clear here is that I do not think that you can 'copy and paste' business models. I do not think that things work like that," Kunal said. "Chinese e-commerce is a source of inspiration, but it is not a format that can be simply imposed on any market. You have to grow it from within. So you can be inspired by it, but you have to develop it together with the ecosystem that you are building," added William.

So if you cannot simply "copy and paste" models and instead have to localize them, as Kunal did in India and William did in Indonesia, will these localized models eventually have a life of their own? Kunal believes that, "In India, the next phase of the C2C (consumer to consumer) marketplace model, like eBay and Taobao, is the B2C (business to consumer) model adopted by Alibaba with Tmall after Taobao's success."

William seemed to agree, giving me an example that seems drawn from the famous videogame SimCity. "I really like how visionary Jack Ma is. When the market expectation increases you need to serve this market with a different kind of product. That is why he came up with Tmall. Brands that grew together with Taobao have moved to Tmall. In a sense it is like building a big city with a lot of stores. Some stores become more famous and you group them in shopping malls where you can find more reputable merchants. As a consumer you have a choice. Sometimes you go to the traditional shops and sometimes you go to the big malls. This is what our model will look like."

Quintessentially East-Commerce

Violette has been saving some major purchases for Singles Day. She has needed a new smartphone for a while and she knows that on November 11 she can take advantage of the hefty discounts offered on nearly all of China's e-commerce sites. She is curious about a particular phone, Xiaomi, China's latest bestseller. She has learned that the phone can only be purchased during flash sales and Singles Day is one of those. It is 10:30 a.m. and she has just gone to the Starbucks in her building to buy a latte. While waiting for her drink, she unlocks her iPad mini and connects to the coffee shop Wi-Fi. She logs on to mi.com, Xiaomi's official website and one of China's biggest e-commerce platforms. Violette likes the website even though she finds it unusual. Websites in China are normally crowded and full of pop up pages, but the Xiaomi flagship site is neat. She checks the prices of the different models and finds them very competitive. The latest model seems fast and she likes the design and the screen size. She places the order and knows that within 24 hours she will receive her new phone. Violette is one of the 1.16 million people who purchased a Xiaomi phone on Singles Day.

China Singles Day 2014 broke a new record. In just 24 hours Alibaba sold 9.3 billion USD up from 5.8 billion USD the previous year. Cyber Monday, which is the equivalent in the U.S., totaled "just" 2 billion USD, nearly five times less than China. Xiaomi has also established its own record. Hugo Barra, VP of Xiaomi Global, tweeted that the company sold 254 million USD of phones in just 24 hours.

Xiaomi is an example of how East-Commerce is not only inspiring Asia, but has much more ambitious plans. In the recent article in the *Financial Times*, Xiaomi's founder, Lei Jun, talked about his newest goal, to take Xiaomi ". . . beyond China and into Brazil, Mexico, Russia, Turkey, India and five countries in Southeast Asia."[6] According to Kunal, "India is leapfrogging PCs at an even faster rate than China and is arriving to mobile's vast diffusion sooner." He means that in emerging markets, people prefer to access the Internet using mobile phones and smart devices as soon as connectivity becomes available. This means that we are on the verge of an exponential growth in mobile connectivity and Xiaomi intends to be at the crossroads.

In 2014, the company began exporting to ten Asian countries and it did so because its developing market strategy is the same as China's.

"Our model is the same everywhere," said Hugo at the 2014 Startup Asia Jakarta conference. "We are using a flash sales model that works very well throughout all these markets." Looking at India and Indonesia, Hugo believes that there are many commonalities between the two markets. "The Xiaomi model works very well in India and South East Asia because the passion in the community is very high." He gives an example of what happed to him one night in Mumbai when he posted Xiaomi's pizza party invitation on Facebook and 68 people showed up. Xiaomi's ambitions are bigger than just selling phones. Hugo wants to be clear about this. "We are now investing in several startups in Asia as we want to be part of a startup ecosystem. We want to work closely with the local ecosystem and with companies whose services can one day be integrated in our products."

Xiaomi's model, a mix between an e-commerce platform, a software company and hardware company, proves that after having successfully produced hardware for the entire world, China is now trying to control the entire value chain selling a comprehensive solution made entirely in China and no longer dependent on Western models. By doing so, Xiaomi is another example of the China e-commerce model spreading out into the world and quintessentially East-Commerce.

East-Commerce is not only the developing world model, it is also moving West where it is inspiring existing business models. For example, Facebook bought WhatsApp to create a service more similar to WeChat. Twitter has been adding images to its application similar to Weibo, China's microblog. The acquisition by Alibaba of the U.S. e-commerce site 11 Main is one of the first attempts for East-Commerce to enter the U.S. According to Porter, "Small retailers in niche products are not very well served online in the U.S. and Amazon and eBay left a hole there. I am not very sure whether Alibaba will serve them well, but I would think there is a room there for a marketplace version."

Before finishing our interview, William asked me what my answer would be to Peter Thiel's first question: "What important truth do very few people agree with you on?" My answer was that for the first time a new Internet model, which was not developed in the U.S., is about to compete at the same level with the developed world model.

Throughout my research, my aim has been to place China's Internet and e-commerce in a much broader context, and observe how they might evolve in the near future. What is becoming more obvious is that China is connecting itself to the rest of the world because it needs to grow. In fact, to support its population and sustain its future, China needs to upgrade the life of its middle class and internationalize its small and medium companies.

Where do Internet and e-commerce fit in all this? There is a Chinese saying *yi shi er niao* that literally translates to "one stone two birds." East-Commerce is becoming a strategic tool for China's sustainable growth. It is the stone that kills the two birds. Chinese e-commerce makes the economy more competitive and efficient allowing people to buy more. At the same time, it allows Chinese enterprises to connect more effectively with the rest of the world and sell more. However, there is a catch and this is the variable in my answer. The speed at which China will be able to reach its growth goal depends on how well it can master the opposing forces of an internal demand and external obligations. The balancing of the rapid internal growth with an international strategy will require sophistication and experience, which take time to develop.

But how is China connecting itself to the rest of the world? The story that I am about to tell describes one way China is internationalizing its commerce while stimulating its internal demand.

CHAPTER 8

The Connected Brand

Shelby 2013. 12.11 西信记

"**A** thousand thoughts run through my mind." This is what Luca realizes during his five-kilometer morning jog training for the triathlon. Out of the three disciplines that make up the competition, running is definitely when his mind has more time to run free. His morning route consists of a mix of city roads and a trail across the park. He starts from an area just outside the center of Shanghai, then heads to the Jing'an financial district, turns into the park by a Buddhist temple and finally heads back home. The park is right by his office and when he enters the gate, around 6:30 a.m., lights are already brightening the lobby. Today, among the many thoughts in his head, he ponders how quickly the market has changed since he started managing a well-known Italian fashion brand a few years ago. The company has done very well, but new challenges are waiting, requiring a different approach. It feels like yesterday when Luca asked his long-term assistant to launch the China startup with him. Just a few years ago, they started from zero and did not even have an office. It was definitely a challenging task, but at least back then things were moving at a manageable pace, although much faster than in the West. E-commerce has changed everything. Luca feels that speed is now increasing at the same rate as the numbers on his bike's display when he is descending the mountain of Shishan, just outside Shanghai. Decisions must be taken quickly, without fear of sudden changes of direction and trying not to go off track.

Before the advent of e-commerce there were mainly two options to sell in China. The first was to license the brand to a local distributor. The second was to directly control the distribution, opening an office and mono brand stores. Whichever way, during this "honeymoon" stage, the pattern was clear: products were sold to Chinese consumers in stores in China, normally in the city center, at a predetermined price. Now, everything has changed. The Internet has created a new sales channel, eliminating physical and geographical boundaries. Furthermore, millions of Chinese tourists are now shopping around the world. Simply put, buyers can now access products through multiple channels. Although this apparently sounds very positive— more channels equal more purchases—it really is not all gold that glitters. Multiple channels have allowed the Chinese to compare prices, realizing that often the very same products bought abroad are much cheaper than those imported in China. Long lines have formed at airports all around the world where Chinese tourists are now claiming their VAT tax refunds. To make things worse, the arrival of a new phenomenon called cross-border e-commerce is throwing fuel on the fire. Launched by Alibaba through its platform Tmall Global, this new type of e-commerce allows Chinese consumers to purchase products from abroad without leaving their sofas. Again, some of these are the very same products sold in China, but at a cheaper price. This has weighed on sales of luxury brands in China, which have begun to decline. It appears that products now have two prices: imported products and products purchased from abroad. A gigantic online parallel market was born and products margins are shrinking.

Companies are now asking: What is the most effective strategy to sell to Chinese consumers? It is obvious that, with the arrival of e-commerce, social networks and global Chinese tourism, companies should create a system combining these aspects. It is now necessary to build what I call a Connected Brand.

After checking his intermediate times on the iPhone, Luca thinks about the right pace to keep, not only for a good performance in the race, but also to maintain the success that he and his team have built over the years.

The Beginning

During my journey through China e-commerce my aim was not only to decipher how this works, but also to learn what is now a viable strategy for a foreign brand to succeed in China. During one of my interviews in Shanghai, I met Luca, a senior manager with extensive experience in the Chinese luxury market. Luca and I have been exchanging opinions and notes on how e-commerce is evolving and how to build a successful strategy for Chinese consumers. He has decided to share his experience, but asked to retain discretion on the names of his co-workers and the company he is managing. Therefore, I have changed the names but have kept the facts and the data real. For simplicity, I decided to call his company the Brand.

The Brand operates in the fashion industry and is a classic example of genius and Italian taste. It is publicly traded with shops and offices worldwide and a turnover of hundreds of millions of euros. It is a very representative sample of an international fashion brand operating in China. Its China history began in 2003 when the management decided to set up the Asian headquarters in Hong Kong and signed a distribution agreement with a local partner to sell in mainland China. In just a few years the distributor opened more than 300 stores. Almost immediately competitors appeared on the horizon, including a well-established English brand with more than 400 outlets in China and a Swedish brand with thousands of single-brand stores around the world. Unlike the Brand, its competitors had offices in

China, which helped to boost sales. The early years were satisfactory, but at the end of 2010, the Brand realized that its products potential was still untapped. It was time for a more solid China presence.

Luca and the Brand's path crossed in 2011 when a headhunter reached out and asked whether he was interested in opening the mainland office. Plans were ambitious: the Brand wished to have a direct presence and a new look in China. Before moving to China, Luca had worked in Italy for three years for a major IT consulting company and then headed to South China to work for a leading Italian menswear brand. Luca worked for three years as a supply chain and operations manager before moving to Shanghai where he worked in the retail sector for four years. He had both the cultural and the operational background in China. He had started from below, from the factory, where many expatriates began when they arrived at the turn of the 2000s.

After joining the company, he looked for his right hand to implement the Brand's strategy. The logical choice was Amy Zhou. Luca met Amy, a former colleague from his job in South China, in June 2011 and offered her the job. Amy's choice was no coincidence. She was from Wenzhou, a major trading and industrial city about 460 kilometers south of Shanghai. One of the main features of the Wenzhounese is their strong entrepreneurial talent and risk appetite. Amy was certainly an example of these qualities. She graduated in English in Shanghai, and found work as a secretary in the factory where Luca worked. After a few months she became his assistant. In just six months, she was promoted to the international customer service department. In three years she became department head.

A few years later she moved to Shanghai with her husband who needed to relocate his business. Though their road parted years earlier, Amy and Luca had managed to keep in touch and when he was appointed the Brand's general manager, it felt natural to ask her to be part of the company. Amy was excited to work again with a leader she admired, but she was also aware that her job would be extremely challenging. She had a production background and no retail experience. There were many issues to take care of and she would have to take many responsibilities, among them: incorporate the company, rent an office, hire administrative staff, etc. Furthermore, Amy had just become a mother and such a commitment would surely stretch her. Her very nature helped her choose. She realized that she needed a new challenge, just like Luca. Their careers had followed a similar pattern. They had always chosen risky and complicated roles, allowing them to gain vast and complementary experiences. Together they were a good team. Finally, Amy accepted knowing that she would go through a very demanding period. Work soon became overwhelming. In addition to the activities already planned, Luca realized that they needed to reposition the Brand. In September 2011, Luca and Amy began to visit about 200 Brand stores scattered across China to get a better idea of what was working and what should be improved. During the visits they realized that there was a profound difference between the Brand's perception in Europe and in China. In fact, sales in Europe were divided 60 percent women and 40 percent men, while in China menswear was prevalent and equal to an astounding 85 percent. Furthermore, sales concentrated on one product, while other categories were underrepresented. Luca realized that Chinese consumers did not perceive the Brand's true value. He needed to talk to headquarters and propose the following idea: change the shops' ownership. They should have a blend of shops, some controlled by the distributor, while others directly owned by the Brand. At that moment, all the shops were still controlled by the distributor.

Luca and the management began discussing the best combination. Both agreed on having a direct commercial presence where consumers were most affluent. "Shanghai and Beijing, these must be our strongholds," said Luca. All stores in these two cities turned into directly operated. Rental contracts and staff were managed by the Brand. Moreover, they decided to do the same in Hong Kong and Macau, laying the foundations for the distribution's four hubs. The physical presence was in place, and now Luca had to work on the Brand's perception.

According to what Luca and Amy saw during their trips, the repositioning had to lie on four strong pillars: a new store concept, a new product assortment (then new products in the store), strengthening direct retail operations and finally branding. Luca came up with an idea: find a Chinese ambassador to promote the Brand. He decided to hire a famous movie star by signing a two-year contract. The star and her personality would fit perfectly within the image of a contemporary urban brand. This was an important achievement for the management both in Italy and in China. It was now time to add a new channel: digital.

E-Commerce

By the end of 2012 Luca realized that China e-commerce was growing very quickly, and that it was about to transform the entire retail sector. On 2012 China Singles Day, Taobao earned approximately 3 billion USD in one day. Luca and Amy knew they had to do something, but they had no e-commerce experience, and they first had to figure out what it was all about and how it worked. They started by looking at what their competitors were doing. Amy studied their strategy and visited their Tmall stores. Back then, it was still possible to see the stores' weekly sales statistics. In fact, every brand page showed each product's sales volume. For Amy it was easy to figure out approximately how much each competitor's store was netting. From what they were seeing, having an online store made sense. These were the conclusions that Luca and Amy added in their business plan together with answers to some other important questions such as: *How do you open and run an online store? What is the most suitable platform to open a shop? How big should the online team be? What are the positions you needed to fill? What are the costs and the implementation time?*

Amy learned that selling online required choosing between having your own e-commerce site and relying on a third party platform. The answer to this question was easy. In fact, in China 90 percent of brands sell through platforms. She soon realized that there were two types of platforms. The first, JD.com, bought and sold directly to consumers. The second, Tmall, operated as a marketplace. These two platforms not only have different business models, but they also require different teams. When the platform acts as a buyer, as in JD.com's case, you need a small customer relationship team. In fact, vendors are basically only dealing with one big customer. When the platform is the enabler instead, each vendor needs to build a larger e-commerce team to deal with operations and thousands of customers. Amy and Luca wanted to start off on the right foot. Therefore, they discussed each option very thoroughly. They quickly realized that Tmall acted as a virtual department store. The platform rented commercial spaces, managed the cash, and at the end of each day, after holding its commissions, paid the vendors. Luca was familiar with this model, as he had developed a strong retail experience. They suggested opening a Tmall store.

Amy did further research to understand how a Tmall store operates. During her research she was approached by a type of company called Taopao partners, also known as TP partners. These companies—often founded by former Alibaba employees, or invested by the very same e-commerce platforms—are specialized in managing, on behalf of brands, their entire daily e-commerce operations. Speaking with TP partners Amy learned that to start a Tmall store they needed to build the virtual store, bring traffic on the page, manage inventory, payments, etc. They had to choose between outsourcing operations to a TP partner, keeping only the key figures in-house, and creating their own team. Amy and Luca knew that they needed to be guided. They did not even know the basic functioning of an e-commerce. Therefore, they chose to start cooperating with a TP partner who would act as their Virgil. After solving this final problem, the plan was ready!

On a summer morning in 2013, in the Brand headquarters in Italy, Luca explained what launching a China e-commerce business was all about. He explained that: "A brand like a surfer chasing his wave. He gazes at the water trying to figure out the ripples and currents. In China, you often do not know which the right wave is so you need to go and try them all because once you find it; it will take you very far. If you wait to catch the right wave, you will not have much luck. In China, planning does not work so well as in the West; you never know which one is the best opportunity, the big hit." After putting it this way, it was not so difficult for Luca to get the go-ahead. Chinese e-commerce was already becoming very popular and talked about by many brands that had realized that they could not miss this wave. The management largely supported Luca and Amy's plan leaving them full independence in setting up and managing the store. At the end of 2013, the Brand opened its first online store, but the wave was not the right one yet.

Despite having a female brand ambassador, Tmall considered the Brand to be predominantly menswear and had it open its store in the men's section. After a few months from opening, the Brand realized that men's sales accounted for 70 percent of the total, while women were only 30 percent. The figures were not normal after the Brand's repositioning. In fact, their offline sales were divided almost evenly. Amy and Luca had to figure out how to rebalance their sales and structure their online shop. They went back to retail's basics. Normally a store is divided into floors, with each floor being divided into special sections. For example, accessories are on the ground floor, menswear is on the first floor, womenswear is on the second, childswear on the third, etc. When customers enter the store they normally go directly to the section they are looking for. Since the Brand's online store was in the men's section, most of the traffic that flowed on the page was male. Despite having a female testimonial, women were not drawn to the shop because they could not find it in their section. After their first year on Tmall, the Brand decided to open a women's store and by the first half of 2015 it opened its second shop. After just two months from opening, womenswear sales equaled menswear showing that the Brand's offline analysis applied to online too.

After a little more than a year since the first store opened on Tmall, sales were going very well. China had become one of the Brand's most important e-commerce markets and the one with the fastest growth. In just three years the Brand had repositioned itself, established its direct offline presence and successfully built a new online sales channel. It was time to combine the physical and the virtual worlds.

Offline to Online

Opening a store was not in itself enough to succeed on Tmall. Consumers rarely land on a page by accident. Tmall has thousands of shops and to guide the public to your page you need to carefully engineer a digital campaign. This was the first lesson that Amy learned from the TP partners. To generate sales they needed to bring traffic in mainly two ways: attend the numerous promotions launched by the platform and create a dialog with Chinese consumers on social networks.

In fact, besides China Singles Day—by far the most famous promotional campaign on Tmall—there are other equally important dates to introduce new products to Chinese consumers. The key to doing well is to understand how to participate in these campaigns. Although the Brand had outsourced the e-commerce operational management to the TP partner, Amy needed to get first-hand information on how to generate traffic during these campaigns. Normally this information is exchanged between platforms and TP partners as they discuss the most effective ways to create traffic and raise brand awareness. Platforms, in fact, are the gatekeepers of every store studying their traffic flow and winning tactics. These data are then analyzed to understand how to create even more effective campaigns. For example, in the summer of 2014 Alibaba realized that women who bought bras of large sizes were likely to spend more money in online shopping. This data analysis was the type of information that Amy needed. Therefore, she started attending monthly meetings between Tmall and her TP partner and taking notes of everything that was said. Attending meetings was important for another reason: the TP partners did not have the ability to communicate the Brand's perception as effectively as the Brand itself could. If that activity was to be outsourced, the platform might misunderstand just like it did when the Brand was initially listed as predominantly menswear.

After figuring out how to generate traffic, Amy had to understand how to communicate with consumers. The Brand decided to open its own WeChat account, speaking to its consumers through one of the largest social media platforms in the world. The official account had two focuses: product and branding. The Brand updated its page twice a week to communicate that it was the benchmark for urban style. In addition, it was sharing its history and its main activities worldwide.

Now that the digital marketing activities were in place, the Brand realized that it should build a synergy between its physical and virtual stores. This trend, called offline to online or online to offline (O2O), is the new key to success for retail in China. The Brand combined its flagship stores with online sales, thus creating a large database of customers, bringing them from offline to online. In order to do so the retail team put QR codes in the stores. Anyone who scanned the codes would get a discount when purchasing online or receive a gift.

Promotions, interactive events, QR codes and exhibitions allowed the Brand to successfully zip its online and offline world. There was now a final piece to the puzzle. However, considering how things were going, this was not an undertaking where, at least for now, companies were triumphing.

Cross-Border E-Commerce

As he runs along the lake located in the south section of the park, Luca reflects on the recent discussions with headquarters. Having successfully established an online and offline presence within Chinese borders seems not to be enough anymore. Two new trends are appearing on the horizon: Chinese overseas tourism and cross-border e-commerce. The Chinese are becoming important Brand customers in Europe, especially in London, Paris, Milan, the U.S. and Canada. Recruiting a Chinese brand ambassador has boosted reputation within the Chinese global community. Sales are increasing too, but Chinese tourists have realized that buying the same product abroad is cheaper. This phenomenon, initially limited, can potentially become a headache. Unlike what is happening to the big luxury brands—they have found themselves going through an up to 50 percent discount to clear their inventories in China—the increase of Chinese international tourism per se is not a big problem for the Brand. There is certainly a price difference inside and outside China, but the Brand is not positioned as high scale, being available to Chinese upper-middle class. Its products do not have luxury prices and can be bought multiple times over the year. Therefore, purchases made by Chinese tourists abroad have not dramatically impacted local sales, which are still growing. Management has agreed that it is simply necessary to provide consumers in China with the same overseas experience and quality service. The problem is somewhere else, Luca thinks. For several months, Amazon has informed the Brand that there has been an invasion of private sellers, wholesalers and retailers trading products online in China and using alternative channels. In particular, they are using the new cross-border e-commerce website created in 2014 by Tmall, called Tmall Global. This division uses a new dedicated platform to provide, international quality goods to local consumers with the slogan: "100 percent authentic international products, 100 percent international sales." Transactions take place outside of China between international brands having foreign qualifications, reputation and quality assurance and local Chinese consumers. The difference between Tmall and Tmall Global is that the latter allows foreign brands to sell directly to the Chinese public without having to have a physical presence in China. Logistics is managed by logistics companies linked to Tmall and the delivery time is between five and ten days. Alternatively, orders can be processed in a warehouse located in a free trade zone in China.

Thanks to cross-border e-commerce, the Chinese market is about to be flooded with foreign products sold by anyone in the world. It is an opportunity, but also a problem for all brands. Why? Because platforms allow anyone to trade as long as the products are authentic. A new chess game between brands and resellers is about to commence. By eliminating geographical boundaries, the competition is now global.

Luca completes his laps and heads back home. After showering and eating breakfast with his family, he goes downstairs to wait for the driver. On the journey to Jing'an he writes out some mental notes that he made earlier on his iPad. As he arrives at the office, he stops at a newly opened Milanese trendy café. The cappuccino is definitely up to Italian standards, but it is way too pricy. "This is the real issue," thinks Luca. The price gap between China and foreign countries is sustainable only when a business is not online, such as a café. But when everything is connected, whether it is a coffee or clothing, you cannot afford to ignore that times are different. "Times have changed," thinks Luca, "it just happened so fast. Tmall Global was launched only a few months ago and it has already become one of the next trends. It feels like being in a particle accelerator. Everything spins so fast."

He ascends 40 floors to the office, greets his colleagues who have just returned from a visit in their shops in northern China, and heads to his office. He lays his bag on his desk and finds a new report from Amazon. He flips through the pages and heads towards the meeting room for the daily meeting with Amy and the merchandising manager. This morning they talk about prices and the action plan to discuss with headquarters. They start by discussing the private sellers issue. Amy did some research and talked to Tmall and the TP partners. Private sellers are individual sellers buying the Brand's products in other countries from wholesalers and reselling them online. Anyone with enough product availability can sell on these new platforms. Tmall Global is a phenomenon still new and the entry barriers are still low. Private sellers have mushroomed. "Why don't we ask Tmall to remove private sellers?" asks Luca. Amy replies that, based on what she discussed with Tmall, some barriers have already been placed, but those sellers who have already opened a shop selling original products are to be considered legitimate. "The platform is simply a connector between seller and buyer. Removing private sellers goes against their interests," says Amy.

The Brand's competitors are already being affected by this problem with a drop in their sales. A few brands are asking themselves how much of their product's sales in China are directly coming from them. In some cases, it goes down to 25 percent, which means that out of 100 percent of product's sales, only 25 percent originated from the brand itself. The rest is sold by distributors, wholesalers or private sellers. Luca thinks that: "If the Brand's online transactions continue to increase, it will make sense to open a flagship store on Tmall Global." This is what he will recommend to headquarters. Luca has understood that selling to Chinese consumers means implementing a global strategy. In fact, anyone who has the Brand's product availability can sell them to China. As Chinese consumers increase, the strategy to create a Connected Brand must include the cross-border e-commerce. Opening a flagship gives a strong signal to consumers and provides an unmatchable service. Often retailers have limited selection and sizes, while the official store has unlimited access to products. In addition, in case of product change, the official store may manage the change quicker. Private sellers cannot do that.

Luca understands that cross-border e-commerce also brings another problem. The real elephant in the room is the price. In some cases products sold on Tmall Global are cheaper than in China. For example, if an outlet buys a product 50 percent cheaper and resells it in China 30 percent cheaper, it can still earn 20 Percent. Even if the Brand opens a Tmall Global store, how can it deal with this? Should it lower its local prices or ignore the parallel market and focus on providing the best service on its existing online stores? The price difference between China and the rest of the world is likely to have a major impact on sales in China both online and offline. Luca will discuss two strategies with management in Italy: the Brand can either opt to have a European price on Tmall Global, just like its competitors, or maintain a price difference between China and overseas. Lowering prices in the short term has obvious advantages: sales will skyrocket. But in the long term, having two different prices, one on Tmall Global and one on Tmall and offline stores, would lead to very negative consequences. In fact, since 2012, the Brand has worked tirelessly to reposition itself in China. Should it reduce its price, this is likely to jeopardize all the work done and compromise the entire Brand strategy. Maintaining higher prices in China both online and offline would be consistent with its strategies. However, if other stores were selling the Brand's products at lower prices on Tmall Global, this will definitely affect the Brand's sales.

There is no right or wrong answer to these questions. There are many factors to consider including an increasing competition and long-term versus short-term strategy. Besides, the Brand is a listed company and its China sales will impact on its share value. It is a complex choice and will require a strong coordination between the Chinese and Italian management. However, there are some important lessons learned by the Brand and this is why I have asked Luca to share his story. The Brand has understood that Chinese e-commerce has changed the rules of the game in and outside China. It is now necessary to build a Connected Brand taking into account all points of contact with Chinese consumers. The technological revolution happening in China is likely to take businesses by surprise if they do not do something about it. Through its experience, the Brand has understood that the Chinese, having not had on offline shopping revolution like the Europeans or Americans, do not have the emotional barrier of online purchase. The opportunity of purchasing at a cheaper price exceeds the need to "touch and feel." Chinese consumers would rather buy two products, and return the one they do not like. To them not touching or seeing the product is not so important. Therefore, online purchasing is bound to grow and will become a bigger percentage of total retail sales. Some say that e-commerce is helping the pie to grow, meaning that it will not affect offline sales. But the pie can only grow so much and it seems unlikely that offline sales will not be affected.

It is true that e-commerce has given an entire population access to products, but there is a risk that it will also transform retail into a jungle. In order to deal with this, reducing prices seems the easier option, but other factors should be considered to build a sustainable long-term strategy. How do you preserve brand and margins when revolutions like this are taking place? Brands should be aware that the increase of real estate costs is putting pressure on prices and that growing Chinese tourism is allowing consumers to easily compare where goods are cheaper. E-commerce is really disrupting the market and often brands might be unaware that their products are already online and being sold by someone else.

Luca's story taught me that many brands will have to (re)think their Chinese strategy. Things are no longer as they were ten years ago. It is very likely that in the future Chinese prices will level. What is certain is that selling to Chinese consumers is not a local issue anymore. An international e-commerce strategy cannot disregard Chinese consumers even though the brand does not have any presence in China yet.

CHAPTER 9

What Happens Next?

Shelby 2014.10.1

If you've ever dreamt of having a completely immersive entertainment experience by simply wearing a tech gadget on your head you now have several choices. You can, for example, surf the Internet or watch videos on Google Glasses or play virtual reality games on the Oculus Rift.

Defined as "next-gen virtual reality,"[1] the Oculus Rift is a headset for 3D gaming created by Oculus VR, a hardware company based in Irvine, CA, south of Los Angeles. To help fund the Oculus Rift, the company launched a campaign on Kickstarter, the famous U.S.

crowdfunding platform, which was an enormous success, raising over 2 million USD.[2]

In March 2014, Mark Zuckerberg announced Facebook's successful acquisition of Oculus VR for 2 billion USD, with plans to turn it into one of their next platforms "to enable even more useful, entertaining and personal experiences."[3]

Oculus is not the only hot company in the headset arena. Another name is about to become very big. About 700 kilometers northwest of Irvine is Redwood City, right at the heart of Silicon Valley. It is the headquarters of Avegant Corporation, famous for its Glyph.

Called a "mobile personal theater" by Reviewed.com, the Avegant Glyph is not a virtual reality headset, but a retinal display. You might ask what the difference is. Instead of watching content like movies or shows on a screen, like you would do on a normal 3D headset, the images are directly beamed onto the user's retinas. It is basically like watching a high definition television.

The Glyph looks like a pair of Beats headphones that can also be tipped forward on the face to become a goggle-like entertainment headset. Connected to a mobile phone through a cable (a micro HDMI), the Glyph can be used to watch movies, listen to music and will soon be able to carry out other tasks such as piloting drones thanks to a gyroscope incorporated in the headset.

Like Oculus VR, Avegant launched a successful Kickstarter campaign in February 2014, which raised over 1.5 million USD in funding. The company was initially seeking 250,000 USD. In August, the World Economic Forum recognized Avegant as one of the 24 leading technology pioneers.

According to Joerg Tewes, Avegant's CEO, "One of the reasons we developed this product was that we saw a convergence between video, data and audio."

He gave me an example. Currently, the Glyph is focused on mobile media consumption. In future versions, however, the headband will contain additional sensors capable of measuring pulse, oxygen, pupil dilation and temperature. It can also record the number of times the wearer blinks. If the user agrees, it can interact with the content provider. Joerg explained that a particular movie could even have different outcomes and depending on the data the Glyph is gathering, the user can be presented with a more customized plot.

Gathering data and connecting it to the grid make the Glyph a viable tool for the Internet of Things (IoT), a trend that is about to take the whole world by storm and where China is poised to play a critical role.

A Bridge Across the Pacific

I learned about Avegant and met Joerg at the IDEAS forum in Shenzhen in December 2014. Jointly organized and presented by Jeffrey Kang, Cogobuy's CEO, and Jeff Xiong, former Tencent CTO and now founder of Seven Seas Ventures, IDEAS is the first cross-border summit on the Internet of Things and Humans between Silicon Valley and Shenzhen.

Participants from leading companies such as Tencent, JD.com, Huawei and ARM, renowned scholars, innovators and venture capitalists met in Shenzhen for this one-day event.

It was an occasion to provide innovators and technology reformers in China and Silicon Valley the opportunity to gather and exchange ideas about the IoT industry. It was a showcase for the trends of the next ten years, and Avegant's Glyph was among them.

Hosted by Cogobuy's platform Ingdan.com, the summit was not just a networking event, but also marked the creation of the first cross-border platform dedicated to the IoT. What Jeffrey and Jeff were presenting was a new bridge across the Pacific, one that will transform technology into a global cooperation effort.

Months earlier, during our first interview, Jeffrey told me, "The IoT is gaining momentum in the Valley and there are many talented engineers working there. However, there is not yet a system to help these U.S. startups to find suppliers, secure financing, or gain access to the Chinese market."

What Jeffrey recognized is that technology is becoming global. He now wants to find a way to plug China and its hardware cluster into the rest of the world, especially the IoT world. His vision is to create an ecosystem to help ideas, wherever they come from, to become mass products in China.

The purpose of the ecosystem is to invite leading companies in various industries to jointly build a complete and open platform, which can help more startups to gain access to resources in the supply chain. It is a win–win for all.

This is exactly what Ingdan.com aims to do. Leveraging the resources and capability of Cogobuy, the B2B website founded by Jeffrey and listed in Hong Kong in July 2014, Ingdan provides a full range of supply chain services to startups. "The platform will first help the startups improve their products, and then it will assist them to connect with other resources within the ecosystem in China," said Jeffrey.

To mark the launch of the platform, Jeffrey invited major e-commerce companies such as JD.com and Huawei e-commerce, investment platforms such as JD.com's crowdfunding unit Coufenzi, Seven Seas Ventures and Qiming Ventures, as well as China's main social network WeChat, with the goal to connect everyone and create the ecosystem.

From what I was seeing and hearing, Jeff and Jeffrey seem to have hit the right button. Technology is now developed globally, and China wants to play a part. Joerg, Avegant's CEO, explained how, in his case, the ecosystem will be the game changer in plugging China into the world.

Joerg worked for several years as Vice President and General Manager of the Digital Home Business Group of Logitech, a well-known Silicon Valley tech company. He traveled to China many times to visit the company's factory and suppliers. However, it was only recently that he realized the advantages brought about by China's digitalization.

During one of his latest trips, Joerg noticed that the process of sourcing suppliers, raising funds and selling online in China has become interconnected. "Before my latest trip, I planned to launch the Glyph in the U.S., then Europe and finally in Asia," said Joerg. "But later I realized that we can launch in the U.S. and China at the same time."

According to Joerg, the ecosystem allows companies to connect with all the key players that will help them to enter the Chinese market quickly and effectively. "Everyone wants to make things happen and it is amazing, once consensus is in place, how fast everything moves in China," he said.

Considering the interest in what I was seeing in Shenzhen, it is no secret that the IoT is going to be one of the biggest world trends, especially for China.

But how is the IoT connected with e-commerce?

The Closed Loop

Listening to Jeffrey and Joerg my mind returned to Beijing GMIC where Marc Ren, Tencent COO, declared, "The future is to connect the offline with online world."

Over the last several years, the Internet has evolved at an exceptionally fast pace. With the advance and proliferation of smartphones, the number of electronic devices that can be connected to network services has increased dramatically. Internet connectivity is also possible beyond these devices. Every object around us is about to become linked to the grid collecting, processing and sharing information.

According to Cisco, a well-known corporation that designs, manufactures and sells networking equipment, by the year 2020, we will have about 50 billion devices connected to the Internet. This opens up a world of infinite possibilities and will cause e-commerce to grow even more.

Bruce, the inventor of the offline-to-online (O2O) application Kaado, sees the IoT and e-commerce as part of a bigger picture, commerce digitization. "Currently, e-commerce platforms have created online shopping and thanks to O2O they are moving services and businesses online," he said. "Commerce and e-commerce in China have become synonymous."

The IoT is on the brink of bringing about another revolution in commerce. "Platforms will soon connect objects to the grid. Connecting people, businesses and devices will generate an incredible amount of data, a phenomenon that is already requiring platforms to build digital highways and data centers, namely the Cloud. Cloud services, the IoT and data analysis will complement each other translating into a completely different and smarter way to do commerce," said Bruce.

Data will be accumulated in the Cloud, and Cloud services will become banks for data. "Companies that store and crunch data will be the new banks," said Bruce. "In banks we keep money. In Cloud banks we keep data."

"Intelligent hardware and the IoT will become the core of the Internet era for next ten years," said Jeff Xiong. Smart devices and people connected to the grid will create a better shopping experience channeled through e-commerce.

But how exactly is this going to boost e-commerce?

"The IoT will close the loop of commerce," explained Bruce. The objects that we wear and use will be the closest and most intimate source of information about us. From our health conditions, to our friends, to our most intimate habits, devices will provide every kind of data about us. Personal data will translate into patterns that will allow companies to customize offers.

"Right now consumers expect retailers to meet their needs and they want a better user experience. Thanks to O2O, they are getting a converging experience," said Bruce. "For example, when I want to go to a restaurant I normally search on my mobile restaurant applications like Dining City or Dianping, and then I choose the one with the best reviews."

According to Bruce, the IoT will provide a personalized and unique way for each one of us to purchase products. "In the future, we might receive information through wearable devices about a promotion at a restaurant we are walking by, or a suggested product to purchase for a specific health condition. Eventually, connected devices are going to help many businesses to surpass our growing expectations," he explained.

This is how the IoT will boost e-commerce and make it grow even wider. Wearables and devices (IoT) will be the sensors. Data will be the brain and e-commerce will be the arm. According to an interview with Jeff Xiong in *Forbes*, the X factor in BAT-X will probably not be another Internet company but rather an IoT company. "If you look at the next ten years, I would say that the big Internet companies will not really be the three you see today in China [Alibaba, Baidu and Tencent] . . . The Internet of Things is an area where we will see new superstars come from."[4]

The Singularity

As the Internet and mobile penetration are increasing, China e-commerce is becoming widely adopted. Given its huge number of users and segmentation, China is bound to develop innovative Internet models to satisfy its disparate consumer base. Therefore, it is likely that China will develop advanced models that will inspire the world, because they are built and tested for the biggest user base in the world.

But e-commerce is not the only sector where China will be ahead. It is likely to become leader in the IoT models as well. E-commerce has in fact created a super-connected world, where the physical and digital dimensions are now coming together like nowhere else on the planet. Through the adoption of Cloud services and data centers, this world has the ability to collect and analyze information on a massive population, which, in turn, allows the development of a very sophisticated grid.

When you add the power of the IoT, with its ability to generate an exponential amount of data, to this sophisticated grid, it will give rise to the development of even more innovative models not only for e-commerce, but also for the IoT itself.

But how is this possible?

Once again, the concept of how technology grows is helpful to understand what happens next.

When the power of the IoT is added to a super-connected grid created by e-commerce, each layer builds on the process of the previous layer, and the growth becomes exponential.

What do I mean by that?

According to Ray Kurzweil, the best-known Singularitarian and one of the founders of Singularity University, innovation is multiplicative and not additive. Evolution uses the latest technology to build new technology, thus the rate of progress increases exponentially. This is called the Law of Accelerating Returns.

Instead of growing in the same way as the other places that are about to adopt the IoT, China's IoT will be more developed. In fact, when the first layer, i.e. e-commerce, is already advanced, the following layer, i.e. the IoT, will be even more advanced.

Thanks to the IoT, China's super-connected world will be even more powerful than what we see today, and its growth will happen faster than anywhere else in the world, because one layer helps the next layer to develop faster.

But this is not the end of the story.

In *The Singularity is Near*, Ray Kurzweil describes an event called the Singularity, a future period during which technological change will be so rapid that it will irreversibly transform human life. The transformation will affect all the concepts that we rely on from business models to the cycle of human life.

China e-commerce and the IoT are the world's biggest experiments connecting the physical to the digital world. They are connecting human beings and technology on an unprecedented scale. Thanks to this fast digitization process, China has decided to take the road of reforming and evolving its civilization through technology; the road of the Singularity. This is evident today with the mass adoption of smartphones and the increasing number of businesses moving online.

A society that was once based on a traditional industrial model is now quickly becoming technologically advanced; smart homes, self-driving bicycles and cars will soon be part of the lives of millions. Of course, it will take time for China to fully transform itself into a society based on the future technological model. E-commerce and the IoT show that China has decided to take that road and the first steps to bring its civilization into the future.

I am not sure whether my predictions will happen exactly as I paint them. However, as time goes by, the trends that I have described here are becoming more evident and the seeds for China's digitization are being planted as I write. I do not know whether China will reach the Singularity sooner than other countries, but I do now know that several thousand miles from Silicon Valley, I have found a place that has created something that will most definitely impact a billion people.

The world should take notice.

Endnotes

Chapter 1

1. 1) MSN; 2) Yahoo!; 3) AOL; 4) Daum; 5) Yahoo! Korea; 6) Iloveschool; 7) Microsoft; 8) Yahoo! Japan; 9) Excite; 10) The Weather Channel. Source: Alexa, http://www.alexa.com.
2. Baidu, QQ.com, Taobao, Sina, Hao123, Weibo, Yandex, Google.co.in. Source: Alexa, http://www.alexa.com.
3. Richard Dobbs, Yougang Chen, Gordon Orr, James Manyika, Michael Chui, Elsie Chang, "China's e-tail revolution," McKinsey Global Institute (MGI), March 2013, http://www.mckinsey.com/insights/asia-pacific/china_e-tailing.
4. Source: www.statista.com.
5. Ray Kurtzweil, *The Singularity is Near*, Penguin Books.
6. "Is Asean e-commerce at an inflection point for eCommerce?" UBS report, June 13, 2013, http://simontorring.com/.

Chapter 2

1. "eBay China rumors," Search Engine Journal, September 26, 2006, http://www.searchenginejournal.com/ebay-china-rumors/3839/.
2. Charles Clover, "Alibaba has single handedly brought e-commerce to China," *Financial Times*, March 23, 2014, http://www.ft.com/intl/cms/s/0/11022ce8-a61a-11e3-8a2a-00144feab7de.html-axzz37c21nNOl.
3. Porter Erisman, *Crocodile in the Yangtze*, 2012, Taluswood Films.
4. "China's pied piper," *The Economist*, September 21, 2006, http://www.economist.com/node/7942225.
5. Shumpeter, "The China wave," *The Economist*, September 13, 2014, http://www.economist.com/news/business/21616974-chinese-management-ideas-are-beginning-get-attention-they-deserve-china-wave.
6. OpenTable is an online real-time restaurant reservation service founded in San Francisco in 1998. Source: Wikipedia, https://en.wikipedia.org/wiki/OpenTable.

7. Kaiser Kuo, "History of the Internet in China," by Sinica, May 25, 2014, http://popupchinese.com/lessons/sinica/history-of-the-internet-in-china.

8. Richard Dobbs, Yougang Chen, Gordon Orr, James Manyika, Michael Chui, Elsie Chang, "China's e-tail revolution," McKinsey Global Institute (MGI), March 2013, http://www.mckinsey.com/insights/asia-pacific/china_e-tailing.

9. "Bazaar," http://en.wikipedia.org/wiki/Bazaar.

10. The rise of large bazaars and stock trading centers in the Muslim world allowed the creation of new capitals, and eventually new empires. In ancient times, Iranian bazaars were divided into two kinds: "commercial bazaars" and "socio-commercial bazaars." The "commercial bazaars" were not the center of the social activities and emerged as a result of an urban economy based on a non-merchant system. The typical and famous bazaars were the socio-commercial bazaars, based in merchant's cities and the center of the social and economic activities of cities. Reza Masoudi Nejad, "Social bazaar and commercial bazaar: comparative study of spatial role of Iranian bazaar in the historical cities in different socio-economical context," http://mmg.vweb12-test .gwdg.de/fileadmin/user_upload/pdf/reza_rezamasoudi.pdf.

11. The Chinese (Mandarin) word for *thing* or *stuff—dongxi*—literally means "East West," and it refers to the two main gates leading into/ out of a market. In other words, a "thing" is something you'd find between the East and West gates of a market, and it is implied that the market has within it any "thing" you could possibly want.

12. Charles Clover, "Alibaba has almost single-handedly brought ecommerce to China," *Financial Times*, March 23, 2014, http://www.ft.com/ intl/cms/s/0/11022ce8-a61a-11e3-8a2a-00144feab7de.html.

13. "How Alibaba's Jack Ma conquered China," Inc.com, http://www.inc .com/jack-ma/alibaba-jack-ma-reveals-how-he-conquered-china.html.

Chapter 3

1. From Porter Erisman's documentary: *Crocodile in the Yangtze*. The description is an English translation of "Il Coccodrillo Alibaba" by Eugenio Cau published on Il Foglio on September 20, 2014, http:// www.ilfoglio.it/articoli/v/121153/rubriche/il-coccodrillo-alibaba.htm.

2. Liana B. Baker, Jessica Toonkel, Ryan Vlastelica, "Alibaba surges 38 percent on massive demand in market debut," Reuters, September 19, 2014, retrieved September 20, 2014, http://www.reuters.com/article/ 2014/09/20/us-alibaba-ipo-idUSKBN0HD2CO20140920.

3. Josh Noble, *Financial Times*, September 22, 2014.

4. David Rothnie, "Malhotra hits an ace with Credit Suisse in Asia," Institutional Investor, June 5, 2013, http://www.institutionalinvestor.com/Article/3214359/Corporate-Coverage-Archive/Malhotra-Hits-an-Ace-with-Credit-Suisse-in-Asia.html#.VpUvik_g-Vk.
5. From "Il Coccodrillo Alibaba" by Eugenio Cau published on Il Foglio on September 20, 2014, http://www.ilfoglio.it/articoli/v/121153/rubriche/il-coccodrillo-alibaba.htm.
6. Kaiser Kuo, "History of the Internet in China," by Sinica, May 25, 2014, http://popupchinese.com/lessons/sinica/history-of-the-internet-in-china.
7. Chinese Internet companies were in fact founded by Chinese returnees with American Green Cards.
8. Kaiser Kuo, "History of the Internet in China," by Sinica, May 25, 2014, http://popupchinese.com/lessons/sinica/history-of-the-internet-in-china.
9. As of December 2014 hao123.com was the 21st most popular website according to Alexa, http://www.alexa.com/topsites.
10. Source: Qiming Ventures Partners, as of October 2015.
11. Lorraine Hahn, "Jack Ma Talkasia transcript," April 25, 2006, http://edition.cnn.com/2006/WORLD/asiapcf/04/24/talkasia.ma.script/.
12. Source: www.statista.com.
13. Source: "Alexa Top 500 Global Sites," http://www.alexa.com/topsites, retrieved October 2015.
14. Source: "Tencent, more than QQ instant messaging in China," thechinaobserver.com, undated but posted prior to February 12, 2009.
15. Source: www.statista.com.
16. Source: "Alexa Top 500 Global Sites," retrieved October 2015.
17. Source: "WeChat Life Report" issued by Tencent on October 23, 2015, http://mp.weixin.qq.com/s?__biz=MzAxNzYxMzc0OA==&mid=400131662&idx=1&sn=9f24c35c801e6ea0a10275687b9612ff&scene=5&srcid=1024ndAyZnmtyX1F8BcLQKF6#rd.
18. Source: CLSA "Building the future," September 2014.
19. According to China Internet Network Information WeChat handled 12.7 billion text transmissions every day, with more than 632 million users in China as of July 2014 (source: CLSA "Building the future," September 2014). This suggests that virtually every Chinese smartphone user had a WeChat account as of July 2014 and sent an average of 20 messages daily. It is simply enormous.
20. Source: "Alexa Top 500 Global Sites," retrieved October 2015.
21. Source: www.ir.baidu.com.
22. Bruce Einhorn, "China's Google tries to move offline," Bloomberg, September 18, 2015, http://www.bloomberg.com/news/articles/2015-09-17/china-s-google-tries-to-move-offline.

23. Tim Culpan, "Baidu's Li says investors don't get China's coming Internet boom," September 14, 2015, http://www.bloomberg.com/ news/articles/2015-09-13/baidu-s-li-says-investors-don-t-get-china-s-coming-internet-boom.

24. Ibid.

25. Alexis Madrigal, "Why we should stop calling Baidu the Google of China," Fusion.nrt, February 26, 2015, http://fusion.net/story/54528/ why-we-should-stop-calling-baidu-the-google-of-china/.

26. Gwynn Guilford, "These men may revolutionize how you shop," Quartz.com, September 10, 2014, http://qz.com/257752/these-men-may-revolutionize-how-you-shop-theres-a-reason-theyre-all-chinese/.

27. Guido Santevecchi, "Non solo Alibaba, I super big cinesi che sfidano la Silicon Valley," *Corriere della Sera*, September 22, 2014, http://www .corriere.it/economia/finanza_e_risparmio/notizie/hi-tech-cina-ali baba-apre-strada-sfida-silicon-valley-solo-all-inizio-ee902fca-4231-11e4-8cfb-eb1ef2f383c6.shtml.

28. Source: CLSA "Building the future," September 2014.

29. Charles Clover, "Xiaomi fundraising values the group at $45 bn," from the *Financial Times*, December 29, 2014, http://www.ft.com.

30. Charles Clover, "Selling to the next billion," *Financial Times*, November 11, 2014, http://www.ft.com/intl/cms/s/0/bddc67e2-68c7-11e4-af00-00144feabdc0.html.

31. Reuben Sushman, "Vipshop holdings: overpriced or a value Chinese E-commerce company?" June 2014, http://seekingalpha.com/article/ 2324155-vipshop-holdings-overpriced-or-a-value-chinese-e-commerce-company; also see "Flash-selling answers the margin problem," June 2014, http://www.fool.com.

32. Josh Horwitz, "A new wave of US Internet companies is succeeding in China," qz.com, June 26, 2015, http://qz.com/435764/a-new-wave-of-us-internet-companies-is-succeeding-in-china-by-giving-the-government-what-it-wants/.

33. Marco Gervasi, "Flash sales site in China looks for a luxury boost with Maserati," Tech in Asia, June 5, 2014, https://www.techinasia.com/ china-glamour-sales-site-maserati-sports-car/.

34. The definition of e-commerce experience in China and its components is detailed in JD's listing prospectus: "We provide consumers an enjoyable online retail experience. Through our content rich and user-friendly website . . . we offer a wide selection of authentic products at a competitive price which are delivered in a speedy and reliable manner. We also offer convenience online and in-person payment options and comprehensive after-sales service. In order to have better control over fulfillment and to ensure customer satisfaction, we have built our own nationwide fulfillment infrastructure and last-mile

delivery network." Source: JD.com listing prospectus, http://www.sec.gov/Archives/edgar/data/1549802/000104746914000443/a2218025zf-1.htm.

35. Source: JD.com listing prospectus, http://www.sec.gov/Archives/edgar/data/1549802/000104746914000443/a2218025zf-1.htm.

36. Alibaba's listing prospectus states: "We compete to attract, engage and retain buyers based on the variety and value of products and services listed on our marketplaces, overall user experience and convenience and availability of payment settlement and logistics service." http://www.sec.gov/Archives/edgar/data/1577552/000119312514184994/d709111df1.htm.

37. Pete Swabey, "Alibaba to build $48bn 'smart' logistics network in China," Information Age, May 29, 2013, http://www.information-age.com/industry/services/123457075/alibaba-to-build–48bn–smart–logistics-network-in-china.

Chapter 4

1. "Cash cow, Taobao. One small hamlet is teaching people how to sell online," *The Economist*, May 24, 2014, http://www.economist.com/news/china/21602755-one-small-hamlet-teaching-people-how-sell-online-cash-cow-taobao.

2. Charles Clover, "Alibaba's looks to transform antiquated state dominate sectors," from *Financial Times*, November 11, 2014, http://www.ft.com/intl/cms/s/0/c24e1540-69b8-11e4-8f4f-00144feabdc0.html-axzz3JTduTiWl.

3. Morgan Stanley Asia Insight, China Retail/Internet, Dawn of O2O—Connecting the unconnected, June 25, 2014.

Chapter 5

1. Source: www.statista.com, "Number of mobile subscribers in China as of June 2015."

2. Source: MIIT of China, March 2014.

3. Source: CNNIC, June 2015.

4. According to PWC's 2014 survey, Achieving Total Retail: "Consumers in China lead the world in purchasing products/services via their mobile devices." Among 900 consumers in China surveyed, 77 percent purchased products on mobile devices. Of the respondents, 49 percent shopped on a tablet and 51 percent on a smartphone at least once a month versus 22 percent and 21 percent, respectively, for 15,080 global respondents.

5. Source: China logistic industry update. Li & Fung Logistic Centre, June 2012.
6. Source: Iresearch, March 2014.
7. Rick Carew, "Chinese taxi-hailing app's valuation soars to $8.75 billion", from The Wall Steet Journal, April 1, 2015.
8. Source: June 25, 2014, China Retail/Internet Asia Insight: Dawn of O2O—Connecting the unconnected.

Chapter 6

1. Source: Mogujie, October 2015.
2. Source: Mogujie.
3. Source: Mogujie, October 2015.
4. Lily Kuo, "How Alibaba is using bra sizes to predict online shopping habits," Quartz.com, November 12, 2014, http://qz.com/295370/how-alibaba-is-using-bra-sizes-to-predict-online-shopping-habits/.
5. David Corbin, "Jack Ma, the C2B business model is an undeniable trend," Tech in Asia, July 15, 2014, https://www.techinasia.com/jack-ma-softbank-world-alibaba-business-model/.
6. Lily Kuo, "How Alibaba is using bra sizes to predict online shopping habits," Quartz.com, November 12, 2014, http://qz.com/295370/how-alibaba-is-using-bra-sizes-to-predict-online-shopping-habits/.

Chapter 7

1. According to McKinsey, by city, Jakarta is Twitter's most active city, https://twitter.com/mckinsey_csi/status/420620928733560832.
2. Catherine Shu, "Snapdeal one of India's largest e-commerce players reportedly gets $500M from Alibaba, Foxxconn and SoftBank," August 3, 2015, techcrunch.com, http://techcrunch.com/2015/08/03/snap-to-it/.
3. Farai Gundan, "Sim Shagaya: On building the next big thing, Konga, Africa's version of Alibaba," http://www.forbes.com/sites/faraigundan/2015/01/07/sim-shagaya-on-building-the-next-big-thing-konga-africas-version-of-alibaba-part-one/.
4. "Konga emerges Africa's biggest online retailer," Ventures Africa.com, October 2014, http://www.ventures-africa.com/2014/10/konga-emerges-africas-biggest-online-retailer/.
5. Timothy Coghlan, "How Baidu is exapnding globally," Tech in Asia, September 11, 2015.

6. Charles Clover, "Selling to the next billion," *Financial Times*, November 11, 2014, http://www.ft.com/intl/cms/s/0/bddc67e2-68c7-11e4-af00-00144feabdc0.html-axzz3LfVdDCB3.

Chapter 9

1. Source: Oculus VR website, http://www.oculus.com/rift/.
2. Source: Oculus VR website, http://www.oculus.com/.
3. Source: Facebook, March 25, 2014, https://www.facebook.com/zuck/posts/10101319050523971.
4. Aaron Tilley, "Former Tencent CTO Jeff Xiong is hungry for investments in the Internet of Things," Forbes, November 12, 2104, http://www.forbes.com/sites/aarontilley/2014/11/12/former-tencent-cto-jeff-xiong-joins-ayla-networks-board-as-he-starts-investing-in-internet-of-things-startups-coming-to-china/.

Index